# Contents

**Editorial**    David and Helen Constantine

# EDITORIAL

Much, though not all, in this issue has to do with what we think the hallmark of our age: exile, the search for asylum, the speaking of native languages abroad. But poems by Ovid – leaving Rome for the Black Sea in AD 8 – should site our topic in a long tradition. The abundance and variety of material we received for *Diaspora* was astonishing, heartening and alarming in equal measure. What are you to feel when an Iraqi poet sends you his latest volume – in English – from New Zealand? It seemed we put out a receiver and signals came in urgently from round the globe. We took all we could of the best and most characteristic writing, so assembling a very mixed company, from Sarajevo via Toronto, from Sofia via Pittsburgh, from Algiers via Swansea. Tom Cheesman contributes a note on Hafan Books. They publish, in Swansea, work by asylum seekers from Somalia, Cameroon, Chile, Sudan... They might be set alongside the *Mother Tongues* issue of *MPT* as testimony of the packed plethora of voices in the British Isles today. We had no wish to exhaust the topic, which is literally inexhaustible, only to establish it as a fact and a constant presence. This magazine will always be listening for and will try to be a staging post for the world's diaspora.

The original application of the word 'diaspora', in the Septuagint, was to the threatened dispersal of the Jewish people: that they should be 'a diaspora in all kingdoms of the earth'. In the New Testament, the dispersal, still grievous, has a hopeful colouring too, in that those going abroad will be the carriers of a new faith. The word itself, in its roots, means 'a sowing abroad'. The two senses – exile and seeding – will be obvious in much of the work collected here.

Translation itself is an act of beneficent diaspora. It seeds the countries of the world with words from elsewhere. Poetry, even in its native country, is a more or less foreign language, a language of elsewhere. Translation sends it down the tradewinds, lands it anywhere and everywhere, as vital contraband. The translation and dispersal of poetry throughout the world sustains an old ideal of internationalism. It makes for a global solidarity against all the ideologies and globalizations that reduce humanity. Poetry is an act of truthful speech, and as such, by nature and context, is intrinsically an act of opposition to the ruling packs of lies. It is subversive because essentially intractable and irreducible. Poetry can't be ordered into place. If it tried to obey, it would lose its soul. It would continue an existence like that of the living dead, whose souls go below at the very moment of betrayal, leaving their bodies to shift on earth a while longer. The Republic of Letters is, in Louis MacNeice's phrase, 'incorrigibly plural'. In its plurality it faces and opposes all fundamentalisms. And it *is* a republic: it concerns itself with the *res publica,* with what we have in common and need for our common good. Translators extend the writ of the Republic of Humane Letters.

There have been some changes at *MPT.* After more than a decade, the administration of it has had to move from King's College London. The transition has not been easy. We have proved the truth of the old refrain 'you don't know what you've got till it's gone', and realise – and gladly acknowledge – the magazine's debt to many people in King's, chief among them Norma Rinsler and Wendy Pank. Norma is strictly irre-placeable, at least by one person: we continue to learn how many and how various her tasks were. But now we have a new typesetter, a new website, a new designer, and, for the first time, a reviews editor. And we hope to appoint a new administrator early in the New Year. These are necessary changes, of a practical and creative kind. The new composition of the magazine – its mix of translations, original poetry and essays, and some reviews – is on display in this present issue.

So much for change. Change is necessary, metamorphosis (which will be the chief concern of our next issue) is proof of life. But tradition and continuity are vital too. With the backing of the Arts Council (without it there would be no *MPT*) we can continue, in our particular way, in a tra-dition reaching back nearly forty years. That is a long survival in the world of literary magazines, and the outlook is excellent. But if anyone looks back to the beginnings, to those first issues in the mid-1960s, they will see that we have a vital origin to live up to, whose premise was simple: Poetry matters. Its translation and dispersal over all the frontiers are an urgent responsibility.

*David and Helen Constantine*
*December 2004*

# An essay and two poems by Carmen Bugan

## Why I do not write in my native language

The first time I found the country code for Romania in the telephone book I understood how far away from home I was. Because the 1989 Revolution began very soon after my family and I arrived in Michigan, the lines were busy and the connection was bad: there was the white noise between the words, as if they needed time to go across the ocean, only to get stuck in our throats. I had the feeling that I had arrived at that place 'far away' from which I was never to return. That experience of distance has deepened over the past fifteen years. Now I can say that in writing poetry too, I have arrived at some 'far away' place, from which I will not return.

Like most people in my native country, I started writing in my youth. Perhaps my poetry-writing would have stopped at some point in late adolescence if I had not begun to write to my father's photographs. My father protested publicly against the Ceausescu government in 1983 and was condemned to ten years in prison for 'propaganda against the socialist regime'. (He had spent seven years in prison for protesting against the incoming communist government in the 1960s, before he married my mother.) Writing about my father gave me a kind of certainty that he was still alive and it was something that my mother, my brother and sister, as well as our larger family, very much liked. Our collective grief was being given words which eased the pain.

In 1985, after my sister, my brother and I were denied access to the schools we wanted to attend and my mother was being pushed from one menial job to the next (at one point being even refused the job of feeding cows at the collective farm nearby), she was 'advised' to divorce my father to prove to the Party that she would not 'pollute' her children's minds with 'anti-communist propaganda'. My father was brought across the country, from the Aiud prison to our town. We saw him being taken from the black van into the courtroom. He was handcuffed, his feet were in chains. Many people found out about this 'public trial' and a crowd began to chant his name under the windows of the courtroom. After the divorce was finished, my mother and the three of us children got separated from each other: we were all dazed. I don't remember which buses each of us took home but my mother asked me to wash the windows in the kitchen. I wrote about the divorce with my fingers on the dust of the window. Then she asked me to put it on paper. I guess that might have been one time when I knew that writing was 'important' for keeping the day alive in our minds. So I tried to be as faithful as I could to the experience and to what I was feeling. I must have been fifteen years old. When we left the country, my little notebook with what might be called the root of my book *Crossing the Carpathians,* was confiscated.

My experience of writing poetry in English can best be explained by telling you about the making of the poem about my parents' divorce. In Romanian, years ago, I called it 'Divortul' or 'The Divorce'. When I began dreaming in English and when the words started to come to me in English, I felt an undercurrent of newness inside. There was freedom and exhilaration: my tongue was slowly getting untied and I wanted to see what it all sounded like in my new language. First I wrote what I remembered of the poem in Romanian and then I tried to translate it: it was called, successively, 'The Courtroom', 'An Oath of Love' and finally 'The Divorce'. Many of the first English versions had too many explanations in them: why my mother was forced to divorce, what happened in the courtroom – as though the whole history of the country needed to be told just so that the poetry itself could come through. Then, as I got more settled in my 'far away' place, I learned how the narrative could be put into images which conjure back the narratives. And so it happened with many other poems, until the English language began to thrill me with its sounds and the Romanian words never returned to translate the poems back. Lately I think that it would take much effort to put the culture I am writing from now into the Romanian culture I had left just before the Revolution. And if I tried to write in Romanian now, it would be more like going back home on an old (linguistic) map.

But there is more to it than that. People ask me so often why I do not write in Romanian that I think about it long and hard. First, I do not want to write in the language in which my family suffered interrogations, prison visits, threats of all kinds. I certainly do not want to remember all the times when we wrote to each other and burned our words: we were surveyed twenty-four hours a day for the last five years that I lived in my country and everything we said was recorded by microphones set up around the house. I hated subtexts, lies, the fear of words. Now I belong to those people who write in a *learned* language. And I belong to those who strive to define their responsibilities as people who were born in one country and live quite willingly in another. This might seem to many the kind of thing one 'grows out' of. But the reason why one writes in one's native language, from exile, is that the native language has beauty and truth in it. Poets write in their native language to remember the warmth of their home, the customs of their villages and towns, their happy youth. They want to recreate a sense of home, a warm cocoon around the icy experience of exile. But my exile is my cocoon. I like it here in English more than I like remembering kids calling me 'daughter of criminal' in my native language: that never sounded safe or good or home. When I stopped looking behind my back to see if anyone was following me to harm me, I stopped looking at writing poetry in my native language. I think the poems themselves make my choice seem less harsh or less impertinent. In my situation it is not that bad to be on the side of forgetting.

### Fortune-telling poem

1.
She wheeled her pleated
And frilled skirt
Right through
The wooden gates.

Red-orange-blue
Dervish-woman.

She had the lips
Of one who lies
For happiness.

A red ribbon
And silver coins were woven
In her braids.

Her beauty was her wealth
And she charmed me.

2.
After she told my fortune
She said to the wind, 'unbraid my hair,
Loosen the coins from my head,
Free me from telling lies to those who need them.'

So the wind wound her in his arms
As he does with the willows
And a pile of coins sounded on the ground like bells.

Poor prophetess without her lies,
She ran along the river.

I followed her
With a good-luck coin pressed in my palm:

As we crossed the water
I could not remember the fortune she told me
And without illusions, tears
Fell to the ground like bells.

### Portrait
He often talks of mountains and itinerant
Youth, years of driving movie reels

Up empty roads, to peasants' hamlets, where
They drank *tuica*, wore flower-embroidered shirts.

At painted monasteries the wooden *toaca*
Sounded first in the heads of rain-washed saints

Then rolled through haystacks down in the valleys
And narrow streets with smiling old men.

I know he left a harsh father, his carpenter shop—
The dogs took him as far as the last house of his village; then

Sadness and rented rooms, he talked with the blind wind,
Prayed for one smile in the blueness of his father's eyes.

Then politics and prison, and I know there
He whistled through the visor in the door
In the bowels of the stone, the pitch of interrogation rooms.

Life of the Black Sea after that: the woman he loved
The children, roads lined with walnut trees – he drove us –
A cigarette in his hand.

And suddenly I see us fifteen years ago:
Helen Street, Grand Rapids, Michigan
Nights we all danced and wept with happiness and freedom,

Mom singing at the stove, brother and sister practising grammar,
The five of us like fingers to a hand. We saw America:
We repaired TVs discarded on the street,

Each of us had a TV in our room and movies
And dreams we planned
To bring through once we'd learned English.

His soul at sixty-nine is like the mild sun
On the window, warming up the house,
And America now is at war with all its dreams.

# Fifteen *Tristichs* by Yannis Ritsos

translated and introduced by David Harsent

**Yannis Ritsos** (1909–1990) was, and remains, one of the most significant voices in world poetry. A prolific writer, he published well over a hundred collections in a lifetime that was, by any standards, turbulent. His childhood was marked by the financial ruin of his family, the early deaths of his mother and brother from tuberculosis and the confinement of his father in a mental hospital. Later, Ritsos was to spend four years in a sanatorium, having also contracted tuberculosis.

He was a declared Communist, one of the reasons that he was obliged to go into hiding during the mid-1930s, when the Metaxas dictatorship publicly burned his books. Later arrested, he was interned in brutal detention camps, first on Lemnos, then on Makronisos and Ayios Stratis. While at the infamous 'Institute for National Re-education' on Makronisos, Ritsos wrote poems, then put them in a jar and buried them. When, in 1967, a coup was staged by a group of Colonels, Ritsos was again arrested and once more sent into prison exile, ending up under house arrest on Samos.

His poetry has sometimes been overtly political, sometimes epic in length, though non-Greek readers might well know him best for short, intensely lyrical, oblique poems that both startle and compel. They use, for the most part, an unadorned vocabulary to construct an imaginative world that is all the more powerful for being understated. His *3x111 Tristichs,* is a unique event. The three-liners have a cumulative effect: tense, bitten-back, and so effectively compressed that an entire narrative seems to reside in each. They are a major achievement.

### Fifteen Tristichs

1:6
Lemons hanging in mist make tiny lanterns.
Two horses are fetched, a grey and a strawberry roan.
You take the grey. The roan will be the death of me.

\* \* \*

1:25
An insect on the window-pane, a burnt
match by the bedroom door:
something, or nothing at all?

\* \* \*

1:89
Stone angels among broken columns
exchange kisses
over the graves of the long-since dead.

                    * * *


1:96
A train passing a village
late one Saturday.  Indigo smoke.
A lone traveller.

                    * * *


2:26
Look – the new moon has just
slipped
a knife into her sleeve.

                    * * *


2:42
Pi-dogs.  Dusty trees.  A broken
balcony.  A door into the night.
I have set my foot on the stairway.

                    * * *


2:82
She drops her bouquet on the bed.
She combs out her hair.
She strips off and goes to the window.

                    * * *


2:85
Each night, as you close your eyes, the unnameable
stands naked by your bed.  It gazes
down at you and tells you everything.

                    * * *


3:10
Leaves step lightly on the nightwind;
in my sleep I hear them
and follow down to the taproot.

                    * * *

3:14
The station at night: silent, dark, deserted.
The station-master lights a cigarette.
He unzips and pisses down onto the tracks.

* * *

3:20
A closed house. A staircase.
A goldfish swims
in the tarnished mirror.

* * *

3:46
I flipped my cigarette-butt out of the window
into the cistern. Is it still glowing
or is that a shooting star?

* * *

3:61
Your sleep – a quiet lake.
A deer stoops to drink. I stoop
to drink.

* * *

3:89
The windows shuttered, the house empty apart
from the sleek and naked
absence of your body on the bed.

* * *

3:97
Those starlit nights... You could hear the apples
falling into the damp grass.
We let the apples lie, but gathered up the sound.

# Three Poems from *Legion* by David Harsent

### Toffee

There was a man who made toffee; he would leave it to cool
on a blue-veined marble slab by the open window
of his shop, which was little more than a tin-and-timber lean-to
in the Street of Songs. There was a man who made small
animals and the like — horses, mostly — from scraps of steel
the plough turned up: high-grade stuff he could fine-tool;
while he worked he would sing, as if he had someone to sing to.
There was a man who made paintings: portraits, as a rule,
of business-men in their best; though he made one, once, of a fool
wearing a crown of stars and pissing a bright arc, while behind him
the Devil herded souls through a *vesica piscis*, its holy seal
ruptured. I thought that if I could find him,
or one of the other two, or any in that street, I might know
what became of my house and those in it;
and what to do; and where to go.

### Honey

With word getting back to us of a very real chance
of pestilence by day and pestilence
by night, the father would go 'on forays' to the ring-fence,
small-talking the guards, checking on how things stood
for anyone making a break for the open road.

The mother braided her hair and laid in food:
he was the pioneer, she was the goodwife,
him with his father's rook-gun, her with her mother's recipe
for hunter's stew, with her flour and yeast, with her longlife
milk, with rice, with wrasse, with huss, beef jerky, turkey,
lemons, lemon curd, cured ham, lamb both on and off
the bone, pizza, pesto, pasta, tabouleh, flageolet
beans, beans both baked and green, green
tomatoes, sprats in brine, Cheddar, Cheshire, the locally-grown
cabbage and kale, salt beef, salt pork, Saltines, salt
both sea- and Cerebos, apples, apricots, biscuits, brisket, brawn...

Each day more of the same, with no one to call a halt:
his honeyed words to the wide-eyed sentries,
her shelf on shelf of honey, the 'product of many countries'.


### Filofax

The entire township, heading north in cars, in trucks, on bikes, on foot,
some with next to nothing, some choosing to cart
(as it might be) armchair, armoire, samovar, black and white
TV, toaster, Filofax, Magimix, ladle, spindle, spinet,
bed and bedding, basin and basinette,
passed (each in clear sight) lynx and wolverine and bobcat,
heading south to the guns and the promise of fresh meat.

# An essay and four prose poems
# by Goran Simic

## Exile as a homeland

Who I am and what I'm doing here were questions I didn't ask myself before coming to Canada. Living for a few years in France, I didn't need to ask them because I knew I would return to Bosnia. Living in Italy for a year following the Bosnian war, I felt as if I were in a train station waiting for the right train to somewhere. On my map Canada became both destination and destiny. Going there without knowing English, I doubted whether an expiry date is tattooed in the writer's mind in losing two homelands, the one where he was born and the other, more important homeland, his language.

I doubt that I'm the first to uncork the bottle containing a genie in the shape of a question: How much is such a writer welcomed in his new country? A supplementary question is: What is the average time an immigrant writer must spend in Canada to be treated as part of Canadian literature? But in fact it's the same question and relates to how writers are treated as passers-by if they come from a different country. I can't shake off the feeling that there's an invisible but unpierceable wall between us and the locally born even though I have always considered literature to be a perfect bridge between countries or continents.

Among the scariest questions I have been asked since I came to Canada are two, each laden with a ton of politeness, a politeness that makes Canadians unique in the world. They are:

**1. Do you like being in Canada after you've lost everything in your homeland?**
**2. Could you go back to Bosnia?**

The first question suggested to me that I was supposed to feel happy about losing my bookshop, my family home, my brother who died after having been shot in the war and, on top of that, about the death of my mother, who, though she had survived as a partisan during the Second World War, couldn't survive this horror. I lost the language in which I had published ten books. Books worth nothing because they had been written in a language that officially no longer exists. My country Yugoslavia collapsed, cutting the hyphen in Serbo-Croat, the language we used in schools, and establishing Croat and Serbian as separate languages.

Everything in my life became shadowed by the prefix 'ex-' and it was my biggest loss, bigger than house or bookshop. First I lost Yugoslavia as the country I was born in. Than I lost Bosnia, the region under the umbrella of Yugoslavia. During the siege of Sarajevo (1992-1995) even my city was divided between two opposing ideologies. A Serb, at that time I was married to someone who was ethnically Muslim, and I am now married to a Croat. Most of my friends left our ex-country to become citizens of the United Kingdom, Australia, Canada, New Zealand, some of them spread all across Europe.

I am living in a country in which the average citizen knows as much about Bosnia as about black holes in space. My scars don't cause me pain any more because after the horror I survived I had a chance to choose between walking again weeping or smiling. I don't know who to thank, but I choose to walk with a smile.

That's why this kind of question scares me like a nightmare. After so many years living in Canada I can't resist the temptation to sing the Canadian anthem even though I never miss an opportunity to show my disrespect for every national flag or anthem. After at least thirty-five years of writing, almost the whole my adult life, I am still writing about how much literature, despite different contexts, tastes, and techniques, builds bridges between peoples all over the world, and much more so than writing under a flag ever could.

The other question relates to one I face almost every day. It is about my perhaps thinking of Canada as a train station and I hold a ticket in my hand going to somewhere else. Possibly America, as the most promising country, even after September 11. It was the same kind of question I was asked while being interviewed by a Canadian Embassy official in Rome. It was a question that made me fall in love with Canada. She simply asked me whether I was sure I wanted to go to Canada. It would be impossible to be asked that kind of question in any other Embassy in the world. When I told her that my goal was to continue to be a writer she told me that I would have difficulties with my poor English. A few minutes later I got my papers.

The question of whether one can return to one's homeland embodies a terrible fear that every immigrant faces. Even after establishing yourself as a writer with Canada as your new country, you must be ready to swallow that bitter pill again, the same pill any immigrant has to swallow in dealing with customs officials. Recently, I was invited to read my work in Northern Ireland. Although I am what is called a 'landed immigrant' in Canada, I still hold a Bosnian passport. I sent it to the British Embassy in Ottawa to get my visitor's permit. On the passport my occupation is listed as 'Poet'. A few hours before my flight to Belfast was due to leave an Embassy official sent me a letter asking me what my real job was. I missed my flight because of the time it took to answer that question.

## Old People Travel North

We are driving north, Chelsea and I. We sold the house,
we gave to our neighbours the things we didn't need any more
and then spat out the window as we left the city.
Our fingers are still sticky from the goodbye cake.
We are now driving through the desolate prairie. God obviously
wasn't interested in living there.

'Look at all the raccoons killed on the road,' I say to Chelsea. 'What's so
magical on the other side of the road? What attracts them so much that
they ignored the roaring cars and glaring lights?'

'I'm glad we never had children,' Chelsea says and closes her eyes.

I see her falling into sleep. I notice the moment when she crosses the
line. Behind that line there are blooming fields, maybe children happily
playing on the porch. In her dream maybe she goes to live in another
house and celebrates Christmas with somebody who is not me. Just like
that, she leaves me alone with my question and my sticky fingers on the
steering wheel. She never did anything like that before.

Please don't die here and now on the road, I beg you,
don't die the same way those careless raccoons did, running
to something promising on the other side. In just a few hours we will
be at the door of our Nursing Home. Smiling nurses await us .
Blooming roses on the table of our small room are waiting for us. A
kind attendant will take our suitcases to our room. They are light
because the only things we took with us are doctor's prescriptions and
receipts from the funeral home proving that we
have already paid for our death. Soon the nursing home manager will
come with a bottle of watered champagne to welcome us.

Then we will have a couple of hours to hang up the pictures of the
pets we gave to the neighbours. After that we will be ready to relax,
enjoy the sunset and watch the dying sun warming up the coffins in our
hearts.

But you don't wake up. With my hands on the wheel, I feel the need to
drive over the dead bodies of the raccoons. Trying to wake you up.

### Pebble in a Shoe

For a long time Gordon from Boston was hiding a pebble in his shoe:
a small pebble, almost as palpable as the acne under his beard, as
visible as his boring life. He tried to hide it until a beggar offered him
his stick to help him be lame with dignity. For months his wife waved
the 'Shoe Heaven' receipt, asking him to return those ugly green
shoes and buy something suitable for his age.

She gave up after Gordon's doctor told her that his checkup was
better than ever. No high blood pressure, no high cholesterol. 'He is
not dying at all, after thirty years of marriage,' their doctor said with a
little smile that only another man could understand .

Who cared that the old 'Flower Bower' clerk said  that Mr Gordon was
spending a lot of money on cacti he never noticed before. Who cared if
the owner of 'Gray Clothes' had a bad time after Mr Gordon switched
from gray to brown.

Who cared if his old pals ate more crisps while waiting for Gordon to
show up at a Saturday bridge party.

When did it happen?

It happened the day  Gordon went to buy black shoes and a shop girl
with a strange accent came to help him unlace his old ones.
'What  beautiful feet for running away,' she said. And she brought him
the green shoes.

Only his dog didn't complain about taking longer walks with Gordon.
Not only to the middle of the park and back as usual but all the way up
the Lonely Street and to the bench right across from the second floor
of the skyscraper. Then they would sit and watch the window where a
young pregnant woman was singing some foreign song while putting
tiny pebbles in a cactus  pot.

'Quite different from the TV screen we used to watch every night,'
the dog would say on his way back home.

### The First War Victim

The first war victim was my desk. A bullet shot from who knows where went through the window of my attic apartment and destroyed my desk. And, exhausted, it disappeared somewhere among the bookshelves. I never found that bullet. I guess it ended up in one of the cartoon books I haven't read since then.

Not long after, I saw a film on TV about the Russian writer Limonov shooting from a hill with an anti-aircraft gun in his hand. I could have sworn that he was shooting in my direction. I tore off the title page of the novel and stuck it over the hole in the window. It's still there.

The war has been over for a long time. Instead of marching soldiers, former heroes with holes in their hearts are now walking the street. Nobody wants to listen to their war stories any more. When I was leaving my city for good I took with me just one book, the book with the missing cover.

Every letter that I later sent to my old address, I wrote on somebody else's desk. I am a writer with a hole in his stomach.

Recently I got a letter from my former neighbour. She complained that the wind sometimes whistles so hard through the hole in the window that it sounds like a wounded soldier moaning.

Anyway, she writes, the lettering on the cover is so faded that nobody can recognise either the author's name or the title of the novel.

What was the author's name, what was the name of the novel, I'll soon start asking myself. But still, whenever I sit at a desk the same picture in my mind attacks me:

A character from a cartoon book is fighting with cobwebs and dust in my empty apartment. He is shot with a bullet from an anti-aircraft gun, a real bullet. And he screams the same way the wind blows through the hole in the window.

### Susan and the door frame

At the time when all of us emaciated prisoners of war looked more like
the ghosts of those we had already buried during the war, Susan Sontag
appeared at my door. As she was standing in the doorframe, that little
photograph from the cover of my book grew and became as big as my
door. After that, muddy and wet from the rain, she fell asleep on my
sofa and only then did I understand she wasn't a ghost.

When she woke up, she told me how once she visited her son's friend's
mother and after she rang the bell, Lauren Bacall opened the door. She
told me that at that moment the big movie screen with Lauren's face
became as little as the doorframe. When she left, she borrowed my bag
to take with her. When she came back next year, the bag had on it the
labels from the biggest airports from all over the world. It looked like
the whole world had signed my little travelling bag.
In the meantime, I had learned how one sniper bullet can penetrate two
heads. I had also learned how, judging by the shoes scattered throughout Sarajevo, the feet of dying men get to be two sizes smaller.

But I still haven't learned anything about the meaning of the difference
between a big and a small picture. We stand in the doorframe and at
that moment we are big. And then we comprehend how our whole life
can fit into one small travelling bag.

# Four poems by Forough Farrokhzad

introduced and translated by

Gholamreza Sami Gorgan Roodi

**Forough Farrokhzad,** the forerunner of Iranian feminist poets, was born in 1935 in Tehran. She was married off to her cousin when she was only sixteen. A year later she published her first book of poetry, *Asir (The Captive)*. She was then separated from her husband and in 1956 left Iran on a trip to Europe. She ended up in England, studying film production. Farrokhzad's second book of poems, *Divaar (The Wall)*, appeared in 1956. After the publication of her third collection of poems, *Esyaan (Rebellion)* in 1958, Farrokhzad embarked on a career in film-making. Her first film, 'The House Is Black' (1962), a documentary on an Iranian leprosarium, won the highest documentary movie award of the Uberhausen Film festival in Germany. In 1963 UNESCO produced a 15-minute film documentary based on Farrokhzad's life. Farrokhzad's fourth book of poems, *Tavallodi Digar (Another Birth)* was published in 1964. She died in a car accident in 1967 and her fifth collection, *Imaan biyaavarim be aaghaaze fasle sard (Let Us Believe in the Beginning of the Cold Season)*, came out posthumously in 1975.

In a patriarchal society in which women are 'drowned in innocent youth' and are created to satisfy men's desires *(The Captive)*, Farrokhzad dared to express her controversial and 'heretical' views about the limitations on and aspirations of Iranian women. She described herself as the 'bird who for long / has been planning to fly' *(Let Us Believe)*. She attacked the tyrannical attitudes of men toward women and questioned the issue of conventional marriage, denouncing it as a 'habitual tranquiliser' that drags our pure instincts into the abyss of 'degeneration' and splices two names and pairs them 'in the putrid pages of some register' *(The Captive)*. She believed that the union of opposite sexes is the 'secret loyalty of our bodies / and the glinting of our nakedness / like the scales of fish in water' *(Conquest of the Garden)*.

Farrokhzad adopted an anti-conformist lifestyle that challenged the traditional ideas held about women. Her love of freedom and the attainment of self-awareness and her desire for a fulfilling life made her, to use Virginia Woolf's words, kill 'the angel in the house' and give up the pursuit of the ideal, charming, unselfish and accomplished Lady. She abandoned her husband and son and flew away from the 'dark prison' of family life *(The Captive)*. She realized that without first finding responsibility toward her own individuality, she could not be responsible for others. She despised social and moral conventions and regarded them as destroyers of individual capabilities.

Farrokhzad liberated herself through poetry. She believed that writing, more than anything else, involves constant toil and requires peace of mind; therefore, she devoted her whole existence to writing and, in the process, relinquished the chores of motherhood and family ties. Her true love was poetry and she regarded her relationship with poetry as a responsibility toward her individuality. In her modernist and experimental poems Farrokhzad celebrated women's emancipation. She wrote about her lover who took her to 'the rose garden' and slept with her 'on a rose leaf' *(Another Birth)*. In another poem, she, tired of 'divine asceticism', sleeps with Satan and 'seeks refuge in the downward slopes / of a fresh sin' *(Rebellion)*. Farrokhzad was also an ouspoken defender of social justice. In her poem, 'Someone Who Is Not Like Anyone', she creates a dream vision of a saviour and a liberator who is coming 'to spread out the table cloth / and divide up the bread / and pass the Pepsi / and divide up the Melli park'.

Farrokhzad's poems have been gathered and published in *Divaane ashaare Forough Farrokhzad (Complete Collection of Forough Farrokhzad's Poetry)* (7th ed., Tehran: Morvarid, 2000) and that is the text used for the following translations.

### The Bird was only a Bird

The bird said, 'What a smell!
What a sun!
Ah, spring has come,
and I will go looking for my mate.'
The bird flew from the edge of the veranda,
The bird flew like a message and was gone.
The bird was small.
The bird did not think.
The bird did not read the newspapers.
The bird was not in debt.
The bird did not know the people.
The bird flew in the air,
flew over the traffic lights,
flew in the heights of ignorance
and frantically experienced
the blue moments.
The bird,
oh the bird was only a bird.

## Once more I will greet the sun …

Once more I will greet the sun,
the stream that flowed in me,
the clouds which were my long thoughts,
the painful growth of poplars in the garden
which pass through the dry seasons with me,
the flocks of crows
which brought me the smell of the night farms
as presents,
my mother who lived in the mirror
and was the image of my old age.

Once more I will greet the earth whose burning soul
is filled with the green seeds of my incessant passion.

I will come, I will come, I will come,
with my hair, the continuation of the smells of the undersoil,
with my eyes, as the dense experiences of darkness,
with the bushes I have picked in the wilderness beyond the wall
I will come, I will come, I will come
and the entrance will be filled with love
and at the entrance, once more, I will greet those who love
and the girl who is still standing there
at the threshold full of love.


## Gift

I'm speaking from the dead of the night,
I'm speaking from the dead of the darkness and the night,
in case you come to my house,
you gentle thing,
bring me a light
and a window through which I could look at
the multitude of allies of the fortunate.

## The Clockwork Doll

You can remain silent even more, oh yes
even more than this.

With a fixed gaze, like that of the dead,
you can stare for long hours
at the smoke of a cigarette,
stare at the shape of a cup,
at a faded flower on the rug,
at an imaginary handwriting on the wall.

You can draw the curtain to one side
with wrinkled hands, and watch
rain pouring down the alley.
A child is standing under the arch with his colourful kites;
a dilapidated cart is leaving the empty square
in a noisy rush.

You  can stay still
by the curtains, yet blind, yet deaf.
You can shout
with a voice quite false, quite strange:
'I love.'
You can be a healthy and  beautiful female
in a man's overpowering arms.

With hard breasts,
with a body like a leather tablecloth,
you can stain the innocence of love
in bed with a drunk, a lunatic, a tramp.

You can cunningly belittle
every astounding riddle;
you can do a crossword puzzle;
and be content with discovering a futile answer,
a futile answer, yes, five or six letters.

You can kneel a lifetime
with a bent head, before a cold shrine;
you can see God in an anonymous grave;
you can find faith with a worthless coin;
you can rot away in the chambers of a mosque
like an old reciter of pilgrim's prayers;
you can be neutral, like zero,
in subtraction, addition and multiplication;
you can imagine your eyes in their cocoon of anger
to be a colourless button in an old shoe;
you can dry up like a puddle of water.

Like a bad, funny snapshot,
you  can, with shame, hide the beauty of a moment
at the bottom of a chest.

you can display the image of a convict, a defeated or a crucified person
in a day's empty frame;
you can cover the holes in the wall with masks;
you can mingle with images more hollow than these.

You can be like a clockwork doll
and watch the world with glass eyes
and with a body stuffed with straw
lie for years amidst lace and tinsel
in a felt-lined box.
You can, for no good reason, shout
at every pressure of a lascivious hand, and say:
'Ah! I am so happy.'

# Six poems by Marzanna Bogumila Kielar
introduced and translated
by Elzbieta Wójcik-Leese

The austerity of **Marzanna Bogumila Kielar's** mindscape compels with its monochromy. White, grey, black; chilly, cold, freezing; and occasional red. This stark concentration is strengthened by the poems' insistent returns to the same place: northern Poland, where Kielar (born in 1963) grew up. 'It is the landscape whose pulse and vibrations I can sense in my blood,' she admits. Though her work as a lecturer in philosophy requires her to live in Warsaw, she feels 'an emigrant' there. 'My first homeland is a post-German landscape,' Kielar explains, also in connection with her interests outside poetry: ethnology, sociology, cultural anthropology. She has conducted field interviews with the inhabitants of the area (which, after World War II, witnessed the deportation of Germans and ethnic Mazurians as well as the arrival of Ukrainians and Poles) in order to investigate how these people establish an emotional bond with the space they inhabit, how they symbolically take it into possession – the questions her poetry asks.

Kielar's poems do not directly reflect the historical concerns of Poland (like other young Polish poets who started to publish after 1989, she is freed from such responsibilities – even if she claims to be an attentive reader of Milosz). Nor do they straightforwardly confront the canonical juxtapositions between the cultured and the primitive, as the titles of her two collections, *Sacra Conversatione* and *Materia Prima,* might suggest. Instead, they chart a uniquely intimate territory, reaching with quickened sensitivity for the metaphysical. Subtle and sensuous, they contemplate the strangeness of the world, distrusting its luscious beauty, which attracts but also misleads. This sensuality, complemented by cool, rational analysis, frequently leads critics to comparisons with Halina Poswiatowska. However, Kielar herself prefers to point out her affinities with Julia Hartwig, the Polish poet of Szymborska's generation, as well as with Elizabeth Bishop – both known for their acute observation. Just like Bishop, Kielar is adamant that there exists no division into female and male poetry, there is only good and bad poetry. She mentions Celan, Kavafy, Montale, Amichai and Tranströmer as her 'mentors'. She also values the prose of Karen Blixen for its 'pure, precise language', and that of Bruno Schultz with 'its disrupted, cracked worlds, which contain more than one universe'.

It is difficult not to notice that Kielar's poems, too, disclose – or collapse – more than one universe. They exercise alertness: their meditative calm, luminosity, sublimity reveal, reading after reading, darker undercurrents, anxiety, urgency. They reveal truth about death or, rather, its unrelenting secrecy. Not by chance does *Sacra Conversatione* open with the poem of August harvesting colours, undercut by the concluding couplet: 'soft hills stand in the luscious light,/ onto the grasses, low, death comes down'. The volume closes with 'Winter Elegy', whose repeated patterning comments on the opening poem. 'Winter Elegy' prefigures *Materia Prima* with its icebound landscape imagery. Yet, it is the poet's 'mind of winter' that helps her behold a crack, a split through which light starts seeping in: and the thaw approaches. *To Understand Glaciers* is Kielar's favourite non-poetry book.

### Manuscript

autumnal peatbog – the breath of poplar and alder
shortens; the light grows dwarfish, pale bonsai,
clutched in the ebb of noon;
the wind prods smouldering dry twigs,
debris of leaves trapped in a roll
of wire-netting, as if, voiceless, it pieced together words
in a foreign tongue, feeling
for knotted nerves, hollowed syllables
under the rime

### Winter Elegy

how fast: the calm avarice of white;
a fragile flock of crows darkens, vanishes in the cracks of the road.
My breath bright on the window-pane. Subdued with purple, vast,
wide-open fields. Dried-out ponds, docile
as under the touch of a gentle hand,
as if it wasn't a bandage of frost.
Hills are cooling over the tops of apple-trees and alders,
a window in the distance lights up. Sparks of warmth wander
into the ashes of dusk
and, not thinking, I break up a slice of bread:

we, how fast, into the cracks of time, hollow
and like stone.

### 'The line of snow and light …'

the line of snow and night – sun like a freezing stone,
ruddy porphyry, under the apron of rock rubble,
weathered waste that slides down, piles ellipses

above the horizon; the barren edge
of a January day, frost-powdered air. Birches
drawn in chalk on the snow, left to the rains.
Startled by the noise of an engine,
crows are whirling.

Ice has long fed on water and the marrow of days, it claims
the glass of the unheated verandah; things have cooled down
and each in its mould

is ready to be taken out.
The ice dust sparkles, strews the balcony, from nowhere –
as if in the sunlight a snow bridge trembled, high up,
over a hidden crevice

### 'Silence of a daybreak…'

1.
silence of a daybreak cut to the bone; waiting,
till at least the wind comes back, clouds gather soot, and light
drifts into cracks;

till the least gleam – a teaspoon on a saucer, scattered
papers, bed-sheets. And a dry flame will consume
the burnt-out timber of disclosed things

2.
torn into strips, the light is supporting trees, entrails
of water steam; it dawns. Sun is a mere split
in a cast-iron cauldron of fire –

### 'A flock of pigeons ...'

a flock of pigeons blossoms white against the grayish cloth
of a cloud, over the town, as I'm drawing back the curtains,
and softly flows down:
the day has just breathed in fresh air; naked
– what names does it await now,
in the gray alleyways?

You're asleep, haven't turned your head; your fist clutches
at the sheet, shadow of the night – withdrawing,
it says, composed and assured: 'I will give you back
only for a little while.'

### 'And again the sea in my blood ...'
1.
And again the sea in my blood -

deserted pier, wind, returning touch,
as if it wanted to assure me that I am. Now, when what's past
vanishes in the polar lengths of memory, and up the live landslide, up
                                        the coils of the body
light is climbing.

The sun descends into the languid depth, pressed against its belly.

Then narrow frayed clouds stampede low with a gathering wind,
lifting the ridges of the waves.
And the whole sky hurries and the dark foamy side of the sea, in
                                        persistent rhythm,

walks at the thigh of the beach.
I have numerous eyes, like animal fur and feathers,
the heart sewn in a durable sack, - and again it beats in its bony basket.

2.
Glimmering coal ships, laborious insects, as if their holds
were carrying glitter.

From the seaside boulevard Jaffa can be seen, and the lane where
                                                          we stopped
in the heat of the night. And the night bore us inside
like an embodied dream.

Cirrus feathers over the sea lingering at dawn -
falling asleep, we took its pulse for ours.
The town on the long wave of dunes -

fat rain has just wetted the streets and branches,
sun dipped its hands in them, to the bottom, as in a barrel of rainwater;
car bodies and cedars of Lebanon are drying. Cogs of the machinery
                                           glisten: it turns, rolls
the bones of life

# Six Poems by Lyubomir Nikolov

Introduced by Clive Wilmer

translated by Miroslav Nikolov (the poet's son).

**Lyubomir Nikolov** was born in the Bulgarian village of Kiryaevo in 1954. He studied journalism at the University of Sofia, then went on to work for various literary periodicals as an editor and translator. Since 1990, he has lived with his wife and two sons in the United States. He now broadcasts for the Voice of America and the BBC Bulgarian service; he also teaches poetry and translation in schools and universities.

Nikolov has published three major collections of poetry in Bulgarian: *Summoned by the High Tide* (Sofia, 1981), *Traveller* (Sofia, 1987) and *Raven* (Sofia, 1995). An English selection has appeared in the United States: *Pagan*, translated by Roland Flint and Viara Tcholakova (Pittsburgh: Carnegie Mellon University Press, 1992). He has also been published in anthologies, notably *Young Poets of a New Bulgaria* (Forest Books, 1990) and *Child of Europe: A New Anthology of East European Poetry* (Penguin, 1991).

Lyubomir Nikolov's poetry springs from an intense attachment to the landscapes of his homeland and the customs and remains that have been found there. The poems convey an acute sense of transience at the same time as a feeling for the past's enduring presence in daily life. Death haunts his work, not as a negation, but as that which gives completeness to a life. Paradoxically (Nikolov seems to say) in removing us from life, death makes us permanent. It is the business of poetry to make these mysteries present to us.

Given his obvious rootedness in Bulgarian landscape and culture, it is remarkable that Nikolov has responded so creatively to the experience of exile. A striking group of poems was written in England on a visit to Cambridge in 1990 and he has continued to write well in America, the sensitivity of his language sharpened perhaps by moments of homesickness. He has reflected on expatriation in the following paragraphs:

**Languge connects. Accent divides.**

We know it from the ancient Greeks: 'The bard has many mothers.' I would add: 'Many stepmothers, too.'

Once upon a time, a Bulgarian expatriate told me: 'A bad mother is better than a good stepmother.'

But the world we live in is slowly getting stripped of its borders and the poets probably have to follow suit. In a borderless world our only option is to become borderless ourselves.

Exile, like anything else, is not perfect. You can't be an ideal expatriate if you carry your mother tongue within you. It is not your passport but your language that defines your nationality.

Fourteen years ago, with the Bulgarian language in my head and a pile of Bulgarian poems in my suitcase, I was to take America by storm. I mastered English to some extent and as if to apologize for my accent (which, unlike the language, divides people) I would often say jokingly that I was still learning Bulgarian. America is probably not the most suitable place for this purpose. Bulgarian is best studied at farmers' markets over there in the Balkans.

Strange as it may seem, I now feel that getting away from Bulgaria has somehow brought me closer to my mother tongue. It helped me look at Balkan culture and the cryptic *Homo Balcanicus* with different eyes. I have also learned a lot about American poetry, which unlike many Americans, I do love.

Living in two worlds at one and the same time could be perilous, too. But I have no regrets.

All his life the poet goes after his poem. If the poem leaves for America the bard has to pack and follow it.

*Lyubomir Nikolov*
*October 9, 2004*
*Poolesville, Maryland*

## A cigarette in the late afternoon
*For Anthony Petrosky and Ellen Bishop*

This morning, for the first time in months,
I listened to a bird. I don't know its name. I don't even need to.
It woke up early, enclosing
With song its empty summer home,
Charting the borders of its transient kingdom.
That's how it is. There always have to be bounds.
Water, poured into a glass pitcher,
Must fill it to the brim. No higher.
Dough, thrown into the kneading trough,
Is to rise, but not overflow.
And with the song it seems to be the same.
One bird, almost invisible among the branches
Proclaims to its sisters: 'My borders end here.
From here on all of the trees and sky are yours.'
The day wears on. It too has bounds.
And the clouds roaming in the sky
And the houses staring at the ground
And the churches tolling for vespers
And coming  toward me like a flock after pasture
With horns of gold and bells on their necks –
Everything has limits. And that's fair.
I light my cigarette slowly, with delight,
Because even the delight will eventually end
And I watch how smoke pours
From the slender chimneys,
It flows into the sky, warm, sweet,
But the fire is down there where it belongs. With the ashes.
And when I hear the chimes ring from the nearby yards
And a plane vanishes somewhere behind the mountains
And the tired children return home from school,  I tell myself:
It's time for this poem to end
So that something else can begin. And I put a full stop.

### Allegheny Cemetery, Pittsburgh

The marble squirrel
Clutching an acorn
Eventually will drop it.
The young fog will grow old.
And I, the only one alive
In Allegheny cemetery this morning,
Will get lost among the wet trees.
Who will show me the way
Between these low houses and tall crosses?
A leaf falls from the maple and disappears.
Up the lane crawls a polished Chevrolet.
Behind the wheel – gloves, glasses and a black hat.
Alice. Jennifer. Scott Macintosh.
Moss blooms in the chiseled names.
The cigarette singes my fingers.
I smother it with my heel.

A breeze. The lake's skin suddenly bristles.

## Apples

The apples have fallen and rot in the yard.
And you aren't here.
Otherwise, everything else goes on as before.
The cricket creaks in the dry grass.
The window pane is shattered.
The stone has fallen by the bed.
Shards of glass cover the pillow.

I'm the master of the empty house.

I enter the bedrooms, lie on the beds,
Caress the heavy dressers full of linen,
I smell the perfumes
And in the white sheets bury my beard.
Having removed the mirror from the wall
I wander about the house
Watching how the mirrors from the other rooms
Peer into it:
The pink vases, the blue duck in the bathtub.
I swig Barbados rum straight from the bottle.
I open the windows
Slowly, one by one, I set fire to the curtains.
Come. You'll easily recognize
The red house, up there on the hill in Highland.
It's ablaze.

### Melancholy at the end of March

You too are a stranger, late sunbeam.
You pierce Pittsburgh, enter through the window
And illuminate the dusty leaves
Of the flower asleep by the fireplace.
Green flames dance upon the ceiling.
The dust is visible, I can feel it,
Kiss it with lonely lips
And drink it in with thirsty nostrils.
Random sunbeam, you will burn out here.
Your life will cease in this room
Between the curtains and the empty bed
Among the sounds of falling jazz.
This is the end. The road finishes here.
But now it's all the same to us where we'll end.
Who is whistling among the azaleas?
Why is the parrot's belly green?

## Midnight Parables

The Mercedes ploughs through the Pittsburgh darkness.
A half-moon is in the sky.

'He sent the birds to the moon,
but they returned
because they had nests and relatives
here, on earth.'

Fred lights a cigarette.
He coughs.

'A tree complained to Saint Francis:
  - I have forgotten what I am.
  - Look at the others – replied the Saint –
  - Each keeps just a single leaf
So, come spring, it will remember.'

Fred lowers the windows.
He points to the trees by the road.

We peer into the dark.

Empty nests.
Naked branches.

# Four poems by Soleïman Adel Guémar

introduced by Tom Cheesman
translated by Tom Cheesman and John Goody

**Soleïman Adel Guémar** is a poet and writer working in French, who now lives in Wales. He was born into a Berber family in Algiers in 1963. He studied electrical engineering at an army-controlled academy, where he endured three months in army prison for 'indiscipline' (i.e. wanting to leave). He then spent two years in Paris, working in publishing. He returned to Algeria in 1991 amid signs of democratisation and worked as a journalist for the weekly *L'Evènement* (banned), then as a freelance, writing for a range of newspapers, magazines and websites. As well as reports and opinion pieces, he also published numerous stories and poems, winning two national poetry prizes. In 1999 he set up his own publishing company and applied for a licence to produce a magazine of investigative journalism. Algeria is a candidate for the world's most dangerous country for journalists: 51 have been killed with impunity since 1994, according to the Committee to Protect Journalists. Guémar received escalating threats; in 2002 his house was ransacked and his files were stolen; and when he was physically attacked by men with knives, his family insisted he leave the country. He suggests that his attackers were working for the 'military-financial mafia' which runs Algeria, using Islamist extremists as its puppets.

Guémar applied for asylum on arrival at Heathrow in December 2002. After three other enforced changes of address, the Home Office sent him, his wife and their three young children to live in South Wales in autumn 2003. In September 2004 he heard that his case had at last been decided: the family now has indefinite leave to remain in the UK.

Adel Guémar's poetry is unavoidably political. It can be as brutally cruel as his country's experiences, but its mainspring is a passionate belief in human rights and dignity. Horrors are offset by ironic utopian fantasies and dark comedy. He often uses the regular metres and forms of classical French verse, subverting them with metrical dislocations, demotic language and the jargon of militias and torturers.

## False departure

1

must I eat great mouthfuls of dust
again—standing in for you—
in order to tell those masks
of absence and ugliness
cradled by sluts and marvels
what they don't want to hear
or go away—but where to?—
in order to put an end
to your cat-startled poses
to be made numb for ever

2

I'm going away to where the sun
shines less gently than here
but the very greyness tunes
the strings of sad guitars
born under the wandering star
damned to the end of time
for having committed dreams
deep in overcrowded dead-ends

tell me to wait a little longer...

all it needed was a No
to the high officials
in the watchtowers above!

3

act as if everything was possible
for the child who used to wish
that Algiers would be the loveliest
of all the brides

## Sepulchres

1.

they believe that the rain
will carry our bodies to the sea
making its currents their accomplices
and erase the bloodstains
darkening on the walls
of the old town encircled
by barracks
white with the powder of human
bones heaped up
since time officially immemorial

they believe that fire
kindled in the wind's heart
to burn us
will spare them

2.

do not lower your eyes
before the usurpers
hidden behind the flag
and the rank hierarchy

come the day
the bayonets will serve
for nothing

## Scenarios

I might have been born at the North Pole
and be living moored to icebergs
among polar bears seals orcas and whales
in my igloo sleeping come the evening

to the song of sirens
in the heart of immensity
the sky at my side
touching the most distant
galaxies with my finger and returning
my eyes laden with pure beauty
great mysteries tamed
my beating heart sharing the rhythm
of a thousand suns and seven heavens

I might have been born anywhere
and be living cramped in a gulag
or a camp in Palestine
opening my eyes on nothing but holes
life-size cemeteries

I might have been born in Algeria
and believe in promises of liberty
witnessing the great hold-up
the victory of criminocracy

I might have not been born at all
and be the wind that goes with you
the corner of sky you are watching
tired of earthly posturings
before continuing your journey towards
the horizon that calls out your name

## A dream

the storks have come back
to make their nests on the highest
rooftops the wind is rising
over the blue lake
rocking the motorboat and the orphan
is signalling to you from the shore
through the swirl of dead leaves
the naked trees
are stretching their arms up into the sky
which is watching you smiling at last


(translated by Tom Cheesman; reprinted from *Nobody's Perfect: Refugees Writing in Wales 2,* edited by Eric Ngalle Charles, Tom Cheesman and Sylvie Hoffmann, Swansea: Hafan Books, 2004)

# Hafan Books: Publishing Refugees in Wales
by Tom Cheesman

In 2000 the government's 'dispersal' policy came into force: asylum seekers are housed in cities in northern England, Scotland and Wales until their cases are decided – at which point they cease to be 'asylum seekers' and become either 'refugees' or 'failed asylum seekers'.

Swansea Bay Asylum Seekers Support Group was established by concerned locals to resist the climate of hostility and offer a practical welcome. The committee now consists in roughly equal parts of asylum seekers, refugees and others. We have received some project grants, but our core work – running drop-ins, providing emotional and practical support to 'dispersees', who now number around 900 in Swansea – is not funded. We raise money through benefit events, and above all through publications.

I created the imprint Hafan Books ('hafan', Welsh: sanctuary) in order to publish a 96-page anthology of poetry and prose, launched in Refugee Week, June 2003, with a big shindig at the Dylan Thomas Centre. *Between a Mountain and a Sea* was jointly edited by Eric Ngalle Charles, a Cameroonian refugee poet, Sylvie Hoffmann, a French-born artist and writer, and me. We all solicited work from friends and acquaintances, and persuaded others to translate as necessary (notably from Arabic and Farsi). Sylvie ran informal workshops-cum-English-classes with French-speaking asylum seekers, helping them turn observations of life in Swansea into brief, pungent poems in English.

*Between a Mountain and a Sea* includes work by more than 25 new-comers to Wales. Only one had already had work published: Abdalla Bashir-Khairi, a Sudanese writer whose nightmarish stories of Islamist tyranny appeared in Arabic in Qatar. Other texts are by refugees of longer standing: a Jewish Austrian who fled to Britain in 1938, a Chilean poet who came to Swansea in 1975, a Kurdish Iraqi who had been in the UK since the early 90s. We also published translations of 9th-century Welsh exiles' laments, and new poems by established Wales-based writers including Menna Elfyn.

The run of 1500 sold out (hundreds of copies were given away to asylum seekers). In June 2004 we produced a second book, *Nobody's Perfect*. Again about 25 asylum seekers and refugees write. Several people we coaxed into writing for the first book produced new work: they are developing distinctive writing voices. We encouraged yet more first-time writers, and we published stories and poems by the Algerian exile Soleïman Adel Guémar in translation.

Readers tell us that the books are eye-opening. For the

contributors, the experience is fulfilling. Nobody gets paid. All proceeds (so far around £2000) go to SBASSG and to the Welsh Refugee Council's Hardship Fund, which supports growing numbers of 'failed asylum seekers'. Their 'failures' are mostly due to want of legal advice; they can claim no benefits or housing; they are not allowed to work; but they usually can't be deported.

At **www.hafan.org** the full contents of *Between a Mountain and a Sea* can be accessed, and *Nobody's Perfect* can be ordered. There will be further Hafan publications.

# *Funeral Oration* by Sándor Márai

introduced by George Gömöri

translated by George Gömöri and Clive Wilmer

**Sándor Márai** (1900-1989) is well-known in England as the author of *Embers*, a world-wide best-selling novel. He was a prolific prose-writer and essayist, but he also wrote poetry; in fact, he began his career with the publication of a book of verse at the age of eighteen. Márai came from a patrician family from Northern Hungary (his home town was Kassa, now Kosice in Slovakia) and lived for many years in Germany and Paris before returning to Hungary. A sophisticated writer of the middle-classes, he was at the height of his popularity at the time when Hungary entered the Second World War in alliance with Nazi Germany, a decision strongly disapproved of by Márai. In the last year of the war he went into hiding in a locality near Budapest, but Hungary`s liberation by the Soviet army did not bring about the establishment of a Western-style democracy, only (after a period of 'democratic' transition) Communist one-party rule, shored up the Soviet Union. When the Communist take-over seemed irreversible Márai decided to leave his native land for good – in fact he and his wife left on passports issued by the authorities who were glad to get rid of this 'bourgeois' writer. After some years in Italy Márai moved to the United States where he eventually died, committing suicide at the age of 89.

'Funeral oration' (Halotti beszéd) was written in Italy in the 1950s, in a state of severe depression, at a time when Sándor Márai felt that he had not only lost his readers, but also his country. He also recognized the fact that his fate was shared by all those Hungarian and other Central European refugees who preferred the uncertainties of exile to collaboration with a Communist dictatorship. The original 'Funeral Oration' was the first prose text in Hungarian that survived from the end of the 12th century, a text known to all educated Hungarians. To this point of reference Márai grafts a poetic lament about the fate of the exile who, having lost his home and property, is in danger of losing his native tongue, his entire cultural heritage. His poem can be described as a long cry of despair, reflecting the existential crisis of its author.

## Funeral Oration

'With your very eyes, my brethren, see what in truth we are:
We are but dust and ashes.'
Like pieces of old cloth our memories fall apart.
Do you still have St Margaret's Isle by heart?
It is all odds and ends now, splinters, fusty lumber.
The dead man's beard has grown, your name is just a number.
Our language, torn, frays too; the loved words we so trust
Under the roof of the mouth dry out, turn to dust.
'Butterfly', 'pearl' and 'heart' are not what they used to be
When the poet drew his language from his near family,
And his song was understood as the nurse's lullaby
Is by the drowsy child, who's fractious, ready to cry.
The heartbeat's a secret speech, dreams go the thieves' way,
You read *Toldi* to your child, who then responds: 'OK.'
And the priest will mumble in Spanish over your bier:
'These are the torments of death, and they surround me here!'
In the Ohio mine your hand slips, the pickaxe
Thuds down and your name loses its diacritical marks.
The Tyrrhenian Sea roars, we hear Babits' word and, hark,
That's Krudy's harp that twangs in the Australasian dark.
They still communicate in astral voices, live
In your body's memory like distant relatives.
You exclaim: *It cannot be that consecrated will*...
But it can: you know it now... You get no mail
In the iron-mines of Thuringia. To write they are afraid.
With no *katorgas* marked, you cannot mourn the dead.
The Consul's chewing gum. Fed up, he wipes his glasses.
You can see that he's quite bored with papers, stamps and passes.
He gets a car and a thousand bucks a month. His child and wife
Are photos on his desk. What's Ady in his life?
What's a nation? A millennium? The arts that we inherit?
Rippl's colours? Arany's words? Bartók's restless spirit?
*It can't be that so many hearts in vain*... Be quiet. It can.
The great powers at great length talk on and on.
Be silent and keep watching. The jackal is alive
Whose ten small claws will scratch you from your African grave.
In Mexico there's already a cactus growing too
That will cover your tombstone, so none can look for you.

You think you're alive? Have you somewhere to live? If nowhere,
In your brethren's hearts...? Oh no, it is all just a nightmare.
You still hear the hoarse complaint: *Brother has sold brother.*
A faint voice interrupts: *Keep your lips sealed together.*
A third voice sighs: *Lest those who lament us far away...*
And a fourth rattles: *...are forced to despise us day by day.*
So: *Keep on smiling.* Don't seek reasons. Do not ask, 'Was I
Worse than the others.' You were a Magyar, that is why.
And Estonian, Lithuanian, Romanian. Now keep silent and pay.
The Aztecs have gone as well. Let come what come may.
A scholar will dig your body out of the ground some day
Like an Avarian horse-skull. Nuclear ash will have buried all.
*There* you're no longer human: 'class-alien' you're called.
*Here* you're no longer human: a number in an equation.
Endure these things as God does; no wild conflagration
Is struck from the stormy firmament. Wisdom has its uses.
Smile when the gaoler tears your tongue out. Smile and be gracious:
Thankful, even in your coffin, that there's someone to bury you.
Desperately guard your dreams and your adjectives: keep them few.
Don't squeak when *the boss* counts your teeth like a horse's.
Hold on to your rags, your bundle, your wretched memories –
A lock of hair, a photograph, a poem –
For nothing else is left. You can still count the chestnut trees
On Mikó Street – like a miser, you grasp all seven of them.
And Jenö never brought me back the Shelley I had lent him.
And there is no one left to buy the hangman's rope,
And our nerves, blood and brains are all of them dried up.
With your very eyes, my brethren, see what in truth we are,
We are but dust and ashes.

*Italy, 1950*

# Versions of Ovid's *Tristia*

by Paul Batchelor

About *Tristia* and the writing of these versions:

In A.D. 8, Augustus Caesar relegated **Publius Ovidius Naso** to Tomis (now Constantza in Romania). The official reason was the licentiousness of Ovid's *Ars Amatoria,* but as these poems were published ten years earlier, this is unlikely to have been the genuine reason. 'Relegation' (rather than 'exile') meant that Ovid retained his citizenship - a legal technicality with two major consequences: Ovid's wife would remain in Rome to look after his affairs, and a pardon from Augustus remained a tantalising possibility. So Ovid spent his time in Tomis writing *Tristia:* poems of love to his wife, and poems of petition (aimed indirectly at Augustus) to be circulated around the capital.

Having abandoned an earlier attempt at translating these poems, I recently spent a month at an artists' colony: the Blue Mountain Centre in the Adirondacks. It was early Fall, and my host told me that within a few months the lake outside my cabin would freeze. When food was scarce, the deer would venture out onto the lake, to nibble the lower branches of trees: good news for the coyotes, who had 'better traction on the ice'. The image recalled Ovid's description of the Black Sea, frozen solid, and I began to work on the translations again, this time from memory. In consequence, these versions are loose: I was obliged to fill in the gaps. Realising how much the Ovid of *Tristia* was a persona made me less inhibited about trying on the mask myself. These are the first poems from a continuing sequence.

> My friend, until you have been cursed
> to wander, kinless, foreign lands where range
> barbarians so foul the farmer goes
> with a machete strung across his back
> simply to milk his kine, you cannot know
> time's secret ministries: how it can crawl
> like a disease that steals
> so sly upon a man he barely feels
> its subtle victories; or like an army
> marching at half speed. It's true: I have bogged-down
> in this forgotten outpost. Do not upbraid
> narrowness of theme: I never wrote
> to better purpose than when I implore
> Augustus to be merciful.

I have bogged-down in this forgotten outpost
on the Black Sea: a spit of land, a fistula
in the oxter of an Empire I once served.
In winter, the ocean freezes. Brigands
drive chariots over the ice, terrorize
farmers, raze the homesteads. Livestock
& women are seized, the men are lashed
to stakes, compelled to watch their crops destroyed.
Leander might have found apt use
for such a frozen waste: he would have walked
the Hellespont like a vault of glass, but those old
tales are not told here. Winter is cruel.
I think continually of my last night in Rome.
Wolves move nimbly on the ice to bring down deer.

*

I think continually of my last night in Rome:
upon the bed my Lady, weeping, prays
to gods that – on my watch – fled into stars
while I pace back & forth. I have a list,
but who attends to lists at such a time?
I pack my trinkets & my winter clothes,
my manuscripts (unlucky charms)…
After the worst is over, there's worse to come.
Like one condemned to die, I'd felt so sure
something would intervene – but now the stars
begin to hide & in the market squares
familiar drums begin to beat. We disagree
how best to use the time & have a silly row.
The hours troop by like conscripts on a drill.

The gods flee to the stars, where they become
daft stories poets use
to show their mastery of form;
an exercise in rhyme.

Perhaps a corner yet remains in Rome
that holds in reverence the name
of one who versed with bite:
wherever poets meet
let the best chair stand empty:
let them remember
Naso, who would not stoop to wring
old metre from a heathen tongue;

who shamed the gods with his inventions –
& found men less forgiving.
                    *

Quarantine or quest,
in exile blessed or cursed,
this ocean will be crossed
after our man has lost
everything to a thirst
beyond fathom: at the last
he will kneel before the polestar,
salute the god of this great vast.

Does he recall the aftertaste
of those tears he kissed
away? Or how she blushed the first
time he saw her undressed?
Who is it waits for Naso, palms pressed
together, as the ocean waits to be crossed?

# Three poems by Olivia McCannon

### Mirror

I've got a mirror hanging from my pack.
It stares up at the sky. The sky stares back.

The pretty half of my mum's powder compact.
We left the rest in a heap, ten miles back.

All gone, the powder that kept her young.
Daily facemasks of dust have made us old.

The only thing still pink is my dry tongue,
poking the cavities filled with our last gold.

I can never see more than a piece of my face,
never more than an eye and half a nose.

We've been walking through this waste for days,
wearing the same black as our shadows.

Dad says it must be 40 in the shade.
And no shade anywhere. Walking for days,

for days and our bones are dryer than ever,
we skitter like dead leaves across the map.

With all this light we're lighter now than ever.
Our packs emptier but heavier now than ever.

Every day it is even harder than ever
to open our eyes and let the sand pour in.

Today I stared so hard at the sky it cracked.

### Map

On the day they find me
they'll slit me along my seams
and peel me out of my skin.

They'll dig out a pit for the rest:
white tendons and hashed flesh,
flopped innards full of stink.

What they want is my hide:
they want it beaten flat,
the eyes punched in like glass.

Thrashed and stretched and tanned
until pores show through the sand
and there's five peninsulas to a hand.

Until nipples spread to ridges
and silver-pink scars are rivers
stitched across with bridges.

When it's taut and dry
they'll back it onto a grid,
trace on dotted lines,

circle round the ridges,
add crosses for the mines,
rename all the bridges.

### Dust

Most of my life is buried in that room.
I look in through the shattered glass

and see a conversation strobed
out by the blast. I ran across

this continent so that the dust,
which fell for years, could not bury the rest.

# Three Poems by Yvonne Green

### Taking The Bride To The Hen Night

1
You sat in the evening light, shawled in gold and cream
and white. Your hair which you try so hard to tame
with unguents, was playing around your face
like tendrils of amber. You caught the late sunshine
in your eyes, in the milk of your skin, in your curls.
Then you caught the late sunshine on your swaddling silks
and it reflected into the glow of you, which in turn
created a pointillism of radiance. Who would ever believe
that a London taxi cab could contain such a moment?

2
Last night we dressed in the silks of the orient, we rang
bells and banged cymbals and screamed into the dark.
Last night we ululated with ecstasy and we reflected
on our marriages, on our babies, on our mothers.
Last night we met like women in a harem and my mother
said she envied her friends who were widowed with a hefty
inheritance.

3
It was a night when silks flew, whirling with their wearers,
glistening with real gold threads in creamy whites.
It was a night when girls were to become women
and when women recaptured girlhood. The septuagenarians
danced like houris and showed the virgins how to please a man
and the virgins danced without understanding radiant in their
innocence.

4
It was twilight in that room, like an unlit bedroom at dusk,
spirits darting in glints of light. It was a room full of pasts
and presences, it was a room where a future was being invited,
like an honoured guest. It was a room where a future was being
ignited.

### Border Crossing

The vervet monkey looks locked
in pace and compass. Over
and over again she patrols
the cement platform, climbs
the metal railing and jumps down,
trailing her dead infant, holding him
tightly by his long left arm.
The wooden walls of the border post
snap with the heat, an official stamps
each passport repeatedly then
waves us out of Zambia.

### Bivi

Bivi had a round white face,
and a reputation for being tough.
Her shiny nose dripped.

She was fat and shuffled,
she even had fat feet,
stuffed into her shoes.

She moved about the kitchen
without losing her temper.
She could do lots of things we couldn't,

like, she kept a live fish in the bath
after she bought it on Friday
and then killed it dead.

She offended people in her family
and terrified them with one look.
But my Dad, and her other surviving son,
softly called her maman.

Sometimes her eyes looked nowhere
and her face got thin and even whiter.
If she saw me noticing,
she put a stop to that.

# Three poems by Ziba Karbassi

introduced by Stephen Watts

translated by Ziba Karbassi and Stephen Watts

**Ziba Karbassi** was born in the city of Tabriz, northwestern Iran, in 1974.

She began writing poetry at an early age and quickly gained a reputation as one of the best younger contemporary poets writing in Persian. Her long poem 'Sangsar' ('Death by Stoning') in particular brought her to the notice of audiences and readers. It relates the execution of a young pregnant woman in the mid-1980s in Iran, which was one of the reasons the poet's own mother decided to leave Iran and seek asylum for herself and her family. 'Sangsar' is a superbly achieved poem of political and personal pain and a sustained elegy of harshness and tender language. Her poetry is a dense and open-meshed lyric poetry and yet it is also – if not political poetry, which it isn't – then poetry created from the effects of political terror. Ziba Karbassi's poetry has always been marked by a passionate lyricism and an openness to emotional and linguistic risk: but her singular achievement, in my opinion, has been to maintain a balance in her lyricism so that it is precisely where her language is at its most tense that it is mapped with exact detail onto emotional and physical reality. In this she reminds me of such poets as Marina Tsvetaeva. In her most recent long work 'Collage Poem' she again writes about love in personal and political terms, but now not so much from the trauma of memory as from precise and present experience, bringing together different genres of text in an almost filmic sequence (a translation of this poem is due to be printed in the current issue of the journal *Sable*).

To date, Ziba Karbassi has published five books of poetry in Persian, all of which have been published outside Iran. She is a powerful and moving performer of her own work and has given readings throughout Europe and in North America. She has lived in exile in London since 1989 during which time it has been impossible for her to return to Iran. Highly regarded by Persian-speaking audiences in exile, her poetry also exerts a strong influence in her birth country, especially among younger readers with access to her work, precisely for her open and passionate lyricism and the literal risks that she takes.

(A much longer essay, by Stephen Watts, about Ziba Karbassi's early poetry was published by the Galway Arts Centre in the Cúirt Annual 2003)

## My Heart and the Setar

All these tall men
    these broad-shouldered huge men
        with hair flung off their
            heads

all these crazy,
    crazy almonds
        these black almonds
            all these almond eyes
                all these black, black
                    pits

all of these
        staring
          staring
            staring
              with
                longing

              pits full of lying

through my hair   my body   my breasts

through my fingers
        between my toes
          staring with lying
            falling

And it is as if they want to
        burn and stamp the
          record of their gaze
            into my memory

into me who will never burn
        no never burn
    never take any of their
          heat

None of it, nothing
                no
                                nothing of their gaze will stay
                                inside me at all

Yes my smile is cracked yes
                the backs of my eyes are dried out

                        I have lost someone

Where has my gaze gone
                where have they taken my stare
                        I do not have it any more :
                                vision, and my eyes are
                                        vacant
                                                bare

Where is my
                open embrace
where is my hair
    where is
                my hand
                        where are my kisses
where is the warmth of my skin with
                                my bones

These are my eyes you are fretting music from
                                yours is my gaze

my hands and my kissing lips that you strum
this setar is made from my thigh bone and skin
                        from the tautness of my nerve
                                from my hairs

Doesn't it burn your hands to play ?

Doesn't it burn you ?
                Why isn't it burning your hands ?
                        Doesn't it burn ?

Heat of it
          heart of it
                    voice of it
                              shape of it


                    heat of it
          heart of it
                    voice of it
                              shape of it


                              heat of it
                                        heart of it
                              voice of it
                    shape of it


          heat of it, voice of it, shape of it


It is my heart, it is my heat
                    your setar


          slowly, slowly the breathing
                              gives way …




Note: the setar is a three- stringed Iranian instrument, with a small gourd-shaped base somewhat like a heart and a tall stem rising to the finger-board. The 'site' of the poem is a setar recital.

**The Hiss of Burning**

('the air is full of voices, the voices
are full of air': ZK)


Light this blue candle at the table
One by one take these blue candles & light them up
in the room's circle


A pecking bird jumped out from my poem
and flew round the room
and flies now & flies
dizzying and
dizzier

Watch out for your eyes!


He's knocking off the buttons from my dress
he's unpecking them
I pull all the buttons open


round and I go round & I go naked & I go
round and I go round & I go naked & I go


A beautiful god has become fire in my poem
my voice has become throat-quaked
my voice has become un-tongue-tied
Voice Jazz
Air


Air has been given an earthquaked voice!
Voice becomes flame, becomes fire
round & round naked in the fire round & round
& the voice
The air
is full of voices,
the voices are full
of air


Poem I've become burnt air in this breath-quake

Hey dear kid
      This poem's a fire
            A scalding scar
                  Will singe you
                        Don't touch
                              You'll shrivel
                                    bubble fizz &
                                          crinkle

Just stand there in your crease-calm clothes a long way off
            Just look, that's all !

## Death by Stoning

early morning star
              are you here with
                          your star-gaze gone ?
little wren
              are you staying in the rocks
                          when you go to the skies ?
tiny silver coin
          are you coming up heads
                    when you collapse to tails ?
my always-greening pine
              is it winter when it's spring,
                              will you tell me ?


your sisters are here
              and your brother too
                        and I am here but
where are you ?
              where
                    are you ?
why don't you ?
why don't you
              come and see
                      the red little shoe I am knitting
                                  for the apple
                            of my closing eye ?
and from the petals
                    of my heart
the red little shift
              I am making
and from his deepest bones
              the cradle that your brother's
                              shaping
                    baby roe deer, just
                for you,

and from their hair
        pillows that your
                weaving sisters
                        make
everyone today is looking at me
and their shy withheld charities
            are killing me and
                making me
                            break
                little baby roe
                deer

everyone is here excepting you
whom the flower meadows of my broken
                mind are craving

and I want to make of my holding
            arms a hunter's pit
                for you
so you would never
                ever leave
                        your mother

what am I saying
                little baby roe deer :
            I don't want anything, anything
                        at all
I want you to always be free and to go
                wherever you will
to sit by with whoever you choose
        my free-flying bird,
                my up-startled
            baby roe deer of the white and
                    running feet
everyone is here,
        everyone, but who
                I do not want
                    to see
        but who I do not
                want : no one
        not anyone,
            excepting you,
                only you

I want to see
                    who is not here

why doesn't anyone say anything
                    any more
why is no one talking at all to me
such silences are sharp needles
                    to bite me
and to knife me through my heart
such silence is
          the deepest scar
                    of my body
and you are not coming
          and the sadness
                    is a cloudburst
                         valley-flooding
                              me
and I am not a scaffold to be toppled
not a felled tree to be sunk in the flood
I am only a bag of bones and skin
                    smashed about
and the only thing left of me is the tiny
               scared beast of my heart
that quite simply
          does not believe
               that this flood
                    has taken you


and look,
this is the sun shining
          and this the white lily you used
                    to pour away its water
and this the red little fish
          that last night a neighbour's
                    cat broke the bowl
                         of
     that I wish is no harsh omen
and this the small flower-edged scarf
          you bought for me last
               New Year

and this your notebook
                    that always was half
                              open
and when I was closing it
          a star jerked out
                    and pierced the throat
                              of my speech
and the word-route of my inspiration
                    closed up for ever


last night wolves were howling
          I heard their voices
                    last night
they brought me your torn clothes
the blue shirt your auntie made you
I wish her dear hand had been
                              broken
your blue shirt is red with blood
and I cannot make out its print
                    or pattern


they said their skirts were filled with stones
their hands were full of stones, their skirts
everywhere stones were being rained down
                    the world was become a world
                              of stone
I wish
          I wish
                    I wish
     your mother were dead
                    I wish I were


your sisters' skirts
                    are full with blood
your brother is burning
          the cradle of wood, can't you
                    smell the smoke ?
look, I am not
          scared any more
the wolf of my fear is hunted
                    by the tiger
                              of my venom

and I've become a fire monster
                if I open my mouth
                                the whole earth will
                                                burst
I was the out-breath
                                you were the in
now these words are only words
now my breathing
                                is hardly half-done
out
        there
                out
                        of me
                                        out
                        where
there is no inspiration of reply
                there is no in reply
                                there is no
because you are not here now
                and because you will
                                never now
                                                come
                I know

and everything
                like my breathing
                                will stay half-done

and will stay like that
                until the earth brings you
                                if ever back to
                                        the fullness
                                                of my arms

# Nine poems by Volker Braun
introduced and translated by David Constantine

**Volker Braun** was born in Dresden in 1939. Between school and university - a period extended by the authorities to punish him for his political outspokenness - he did various labouring jobs; then at the University of Leipzig he read philosophy. He worked as dramatist and director at the Berliner Ensemble (with Brecht's widow, Helene Weigel) and at the Deutsches Theater, also in Berlin. He is the author of numerous plays, and of volumes of fiction, poetry and essays; many of which, before 1989, got him into trouble. He has won many prizes, the latest, the prestigious Georg-Büchner-Preis, in 2000.

Volker Braun is a humane, witty, brave and bitterly disappointed poet. He does what poets should do: he bears witness. He suffers the times, and tries to make sense of them for himself and for others. His work has turned on the *Wende* itself, on the colossal shift, upheaval and turning-point of November 1989. Poems of rage, grief and determined hope before that moment are faced, after it, by others expressing an equal disappointment. So much hope, so much disappointment. Wanting what his mentor Brecht called 'a life worthy of human beings', he got first the betrayal of socialism then the sell-out to a triumphant capitalism. As for us, we cannot now pretend that his criticisms only apply to the other system and the other side.

Like most writers, Volker Braun has his own touchstones in world literature, and many of his poems set quotations from, for example, Rimbaud, Hölderlin and Brecht, into his own context, where they work as ironic illuminations of a present plight. Thus in 'The Turningpoint' he includes the sardonic exchange which Büchner invented for an epigraph to his revolutionary comedy *Leonce and Lena*: the idealist Alfieri asking: 'E la fama?' and the realist Gozzi countering with 'E la fame?' In 'Pliny sends greetings to Tacitus', a poem addressed to fellow-dramatist and dissident Heiner Müller, Braun quotes from the letters of the Younger Pliny to Cornelius Tacitus and Maecilius Nepos, and so illuminates the man-made catastrophes of the twentieth century (and his own involvement in them) by an imagery taken from AD 79.

There are more poems by Volker Braun in *Modern Poetry in Translation*, no. 18, 'European Voices'. These translations of Volker Braun appear by kind permission of Suhrkamp Verlag.

## Rubble Flora

Over the rubble heaps the wild trees stand.
From the blackened stones the green leaps up like flame.
Extinguished cities. Fiery lupins and
Widows in the ruins set up house and home.


## An Account of Despair

When she entered
And set down her empty bags on my tabletops
I felt caught out in my
Missed deeds.

The evening news dripped bloodily from the screen
And the bed stood encircled
Aside in the uninhabited zone.

She approached and embraced me
At once as though she could not be wrong

And fastened shut the door
With a black twine that had no end
And took the pictures from the wall, but there was worse:
She took the pictures out of the windows

And stopped dead in their tracks
My other friends
With her voice on the breeze
Of birds torn all to pieces.

I saw there was no arguing with this woman
She is right
Like a ruling
ONCE AND FOR ALL

I saw all the things she held in her hands
And rose quietly like a planet that does not belong
And vanishes from the screen.

*Unfinished*


## The Muddy Levels

The matchstick-men of planning
Randomly inscribed
Year after year
On the tough black damned and stinking immeasurably long
Long-suffering.


## The Turningpoint

The astonishing land breeze
In the corridors. Smashed
Desks. The blood the newspapers
AND FAME? AND HUNGER
Spew up. History
Turns on its heels and is
For one moment
Determined.


## New Wallpaper

The management informs me
The alterations were completed very quietly long ago.
But the premises are no more spacious
The stairs inconvenient
And are the little rooms any lighter?
And why are people moving out not in?

## The Builder on Stalin Avenue

Among the massive blocks
I come across a builder. He belongs
To the sunken classes
Who made walls that were true
And insurrections. Dreaming
I lead him back to the sweat-drenched
Scaffolding
Of a beginning.

## My Brother

The beggar on the greasy steps of the BANCO DI ROMA
On a piece of corrugated cardboard BROTHER, curled
In his cap at noon. How am I better off than him?
Nothing but my verses feeds me and gets me a bed.
My lines, my sores, cover the paper, filthy
And exposed. Shameless words
That live on the streets, begging for sympathy.
A skinny boy with his hand out
Staggers from human being to human being
For some humanity. The gypsies in the exhaust fumes.
Not even by a hope am I better off than you.

## Marlboro is Red. Red is Marlboro

Sleep now, rest ... But you like awake, smiling.
Only my body is still underway
On one road or another and alas where to?
You wanted to encompass the unknown.
I know all that now. All that is the desert.
Desert, you say. Or I say affluence.
Enjoy, breathe, eat. Offer your hands open.
I'll never live towards a turningpoint again.

## Pliny sends greetings to Tacitus
*(For Heiner Müller)*

Why did Pliny make for the centre of the catastrophe
When the cloud rose up in the shape of a pine
White and filthy as the elements it had dragged aloft
*As a man of science he thought the matter*
*Worth a closer look.* He called for his sandals
Launched the quadriremes and with a favourable wind
Bore towards Vesuvius *dirt and red-hot pumice*
Why did he not remain at a safe distance
At his card-table in Misenum
He knew the *true nature* of the upheaval
Harmlessly verdant to the summit, the peasants
Settle in the ashes of their hopes
When the memory cools and is able to calculate
*As you know, land prices have risen again*
Pliny the Younger writes to Maecilius Nepos
*Because the Princeps has obliged the candidates*
*To purchase land before their election*
A dwelling place in the Empire country houses under the volcano
The risks of the political cinder-track, why
Did he want to know exactly *He hurried*
*Where others were fleeing from, directly into the danger*
*Dictating to a scribe all the images of the disaster*
While the sea withdrew and chunks of stone were falling
In his complete *Natural History* (37 volumes)
He had foretold the event and the end of the world
Which now was reduced to his own
A man of my age with an insatiable curiosity *He*
*Had himself carried to the bath, dined quietly and lay down*
In the horror, his breathing, because of
His corpulence, audible
Why did I remain in the midst of the catastrophe
Of my century *The Betrayed Revolution*
With all the traitors who wished to know it betrayed
I thought the matter worthy etc. *They fastened cushions*
*On their heads for protection against the falling stones*
I knew the true nature of the upheaval
Planted with red flags to the summit, the workers
And peasants scrabbling in the mud of promises

I have described (in volume after volume) the downfall
*Only now and then a mouthful of cold water*
And the end will only be my own
Meanwhile I bathe and eat
Of the dross of another catastrophe
*The Triumph of the West* by J.M.Roberts
Observed close up a natural phenomenon
Till the debris reaches the doorstep crushingly
Why do I not abide
At my desk in my certain hope
*Only now and then it was necessary*
*To shake off the ash so as not to be buried*
The steamrollers of progress *breathtaking*
*They stopped his throat* The ash of Auschwitz
The dark cloud in the shape of a mushroom
Leaping from the ground, why do I go on with the exercise
In the cold lava of the revolution
In the Nile mud of civilization
In a four-door wreck of an automobile
In the exhaust fumes of Naples

# Ten poems by Wulf Kirsten

introduced and translated by Stefan Tobler

**Wulf Kirsten** was born in Klipphausen in 1934. Klipphausen, which is near to Meissen in the German state of Saxony, was at the time a rural, and rather feudal, community. His father was a stonemason and the family also had a smallholding. The wealth of experience which Kirsten has from his rural childhood gives his poetry a truth similar to that of Clare's.

Kirsten's poetry is both lyrical and documentary, observing the world very closely and particularly. He dislikes being called a 'nature poet', because he cannot write about nature in general, just the places he knows, with their particular histories. He loves to give a detailed account of all that he sees and does not shy away from using words from his childhood or local dialect, even if they would be unknown or unusual to some urban readers. The baker's peel that 'shoots over the ember hole' in 'Unforgettable Moment' would be a rare sight in any Western European country today, as would the windrows in a field in 'Mecklenburg Summer (1959)'.

Like Clare's, his poetry could never be idyllic. He was old enough to experience the war, the cruelties in his village and the terror of the Russian advance. His poetry and other writing has always been political. He has researched and written extensively on Buchenwald concentration camp and his poetry has dealt with other concerns with as much openness as his East German citizenship allowed. The catastrophe that was East German farm collectivisation is present in his poetry, in 'A Feast for the Eyes' and in the date of the more elegiac 'Mecklenburg Summer (1959)', which looks back to the year before the collectivisations of 1960. 'Flats on a Sunday' gives us an uncomfortably expressive document of forced flat-sharing in a time of housing shortages.

However rooted his poetry is, Kirsten is very much an internationally aware poet. He has travelled widely in Europe and his poetry reflects this. The prose poem 'Luchian' was inspired by the paintings and biography of the Romanian painter Luchian and his paintings' titles are collaged at the start of the poem. Kirsten's collected poems, *Erdlebenbilder (Pictures of Earth Life)*, which was published in 2004 by Ammann Verlag on the occasion of his seventieth birthday, is testament to the full scope of his poetry. These translations first appeared on **www.litrix.de**.

## Lake Landscape

A summer like there never was again.
The only truth is the night-time breath of the lake,
is the language of things, silhouetted in black;
nothing heard even in the reed beds where birds sleep.

For one breath summer rested.
In the treetops a soundless stepping,
summer's path led above walls of cloud,
a reading of skin in the night's good keeping.

The lake a blind mirror,
a pair of words dived
into the water's cool breath:
a foretaste of handshake and scene change.

Two gasps, a passing symmetry, blown away,
nothing is as constant
as the heavenly bodies
carrying us off with their long arms.


## Luchian

The Sad Master Locksmith. Lorica. Safta's Blossoming Life. The
Abandoned Inn. The Cemetery Path. The Ox-cart. Drunk from the
fountain at Brebu. Coloured in the Moinesti houses scattered on the
hill like straw bales. The uprising, smothered in the blood of eleven
thousand massacred farmers. The washerwoman's leaden white. Fleecy
bundles of flowers, shining like enamel, in Romanian jugs. The vivid
poppy flares up. Outlines are trimmed with beams of light. The painter
fixes the silvery grey mist in pastels, it rises in the twilight from the
Chiajna meadows. A pulsating mass of colour, dipped in sun. Shades of
green. Glowing constellations, which scream in anguish. Pain colours
the calligraphy of flourished paint, like a suddenly wild wind in the
leaves that carries everything off and buries it. A person whose head is
slightly cocked to one side pleading for his life, his lips burning hellishly
on the devil's doorstep, who defies death. His body already stiff and
exhausted, only his eye left unscathed. His paintbrush strapped to his
wrist like a spear.

### Flats on a Sunday

Next to each other, on top of each other,
door beside door, wall against wall,
sharing the scarce flats
in the thin-walled house,
live slander greed numbness,
the go-getter, consumed by ambition,
the sniffer dog, who grew
elephant ears.
Othello on a crutch
whose small pension ate away at him.
The fingers of an elderly aesthete
flit for hours over the grand piano
and fill the stairwell
with a shimmering column
of dirt and dusty notes,
while a drunkard
beats his wife and children.

### Wasteland

*For Eberhard Haufe*

Just walking across country, nothing to me, nothing to you, where nothing grows which is of use in farming. A meagre broom-ridden terrain rustling with black pods. There's a grouchy rattling and crackling around this last outpost. Thistles parade proudly, boy scouts, heads held high. Their untamed lust for life taking off with the wind. Closed gravel pits, where nature has a free hand. In the pathless, madly growing mat of grass, the gentians speckle the turf with their deep-blue, autumn goblets. The thorny slope covered with a rich variety of self-seeders. A wall of maquis. No sign: Danger! Impenetrable Zone! No Access! Reserve for foxes and small game. So many boltholes, so many good-nights. Camomile growing lushly on burnt debris and iron parts made by the ever cheerful farm mechanic, God rest his soul. Tufts of wool as landmarks in the wilderness, ripped from the herd by the bushes. Earth over old burrows giving way underfoot. Tracks left by gravel carts disappearing under burrs and nettles. A burnt spot: this is where the shepherd rested after lunch. Above the fertile arable land, dull and level as far as the eye can see, this wild reef rises up with a plume of green bushes. A wave of earth quickens the landscape near the placid stream that flows into the Gramme.

### Self

The garden wall down the slope on its knees,
the gaping cracks between stones filled with elder,
bell after bell of wild hop overran the fence
and tied the world closed before my eyes,
I lay in the grass, arms under my head.

A pear tree was crumbling beside me, choked
in brown rot, bundles of shoots poked up into light,
hole after hole artfully placed by a woodpecker
made the tree a flute for starlings,
I looked into the green sun, arms under my head.

The bramble thickets and the hornbeam hedge
gave the bank down to the river a leafy roof,
wagging imps whirred from the wrens' nest
and darted through my private hideaway,
in which I lay, arms under my head.

A daydreamer, happy to idle away whole afternoons
and intently follow pictures in the clouds,
lay quietly in lazy amazement in bloody times
on a grass-tangled meadow sloping out of the village,
his knees drawn up, his arms under his head.

**Unforgettable Moment**
Summer raises its green roof
over the track through the fields,
all the way to the stony vineyards.
Two wheel ruts run to the woods, cut
deep in the clay.

Mother talking to Lorenz, the baker's boy,
strollers under cherry trees.
My eyes stare at his knee socks,
topped off with fluffy bobbles,
Sunday-white.

Face and voice forgotten.
I paid no attention
to his words.
The baker had to enlist.
He went missing on the Eastern front.

Guided by other hands,
his peel shoots
over the ember hole.
The avenue of cherries has been felled.
The wind has a free run.

I see myself holding my mother's hand
in the avenue.
A shady walk full of leafy coolness.
A talk under a cherry tree,
refreshing, weighing light.

My mind's eye
held spell-bound
and astonished
on the bobbles of that
baker's Sunday.

**The Swing**
From my window:
a girl swinging.
She floats and swoops
absent-mindedly and agile
under the flowering pear tree.
The awkward branches
balled to a bloom-white body
and billowing, buzzing, upwards.
A colony of bees are
bundling over each other
industriously.
Without a sound
the girl floats
over the lawn.
She swings
regular as a pendulum
between earth and tree blossom.
The girl lifts spring
into the heavens.
The heavens nudge the swing
back down to earth.

### Mecklenburg Summer (1959)

*Every place shelters its own dream.*
*Alfons Paquet*

Every metaphor for silence
rudely thrown out and hushed up.
No steps crunch on the sand
of a dark summer path.
Woollen tongues have ground down
the village tales of simple souls.
No torrents of corn fall
from the feeding board into the big farm machine.
No shimmering dust dancing
that remembers:
back then, on the threshing floor.
I stood tall in the husk storm
and pitched down a cartload of wheat.
I pulled the horses' collars
over their heads
and looked at them without any fear,
animals good as gold, gentle
as the sunsets outside
on the nettle path, barefoot in my clogs,
having slipped free of the world towards evening
above windrows, swallows' wings
were flitting low and lower over the earth.
Heaven only knows, look before you step, the end is coming,
the day of trouble is drawing near.
Young lady-in-the-green goes in sackcloth and ashes,
the blacksmith's daughter, in whose
gardens you lived in your day.
What you knew, what I saw:
Old Mecklenburg, midland
pairs of storks, summer faces,
mirror images of mirror images
back to front in sharp silhouette
on the nightly enchanted Leizen lake,
bewitched on an overgrown byway.
All words have been lost with the things

which the big muncher-cruncher ate.
No farmyard gate creaks on its hinges,
no flywheel turns any more,
nothing crumples
where everything has long been smashed.
The crankshafts, the riddles -
scrap, scrap, scrap.

**Anything, Save . . .**
Door closed, time to be off,
I didn't ask what else
could keep me here
in Potschappel, no more trains
left from this rather
horrendous station, dragged
my suitcase all night long
through villages which had sunk
into themselves, walking on the verge
of an endless country road,
suffering the frost yard by yard,
with every step on Sachsdorf Hill
knee-deep in snow,
the toil of plodding
up a road buried under drifts, just
a single solitary thought
kept me awake: anything, save
foundering in the snow
with my brown vulcanised suitcase,
nobody else that night was going
that way, which was no longer a way,
after every step, deep into
the snow, that didn't hold me,
needing to heave a leg out again
and thinking as I did, just get
over Sachsdorf Hill,
anything, save . . .

### A Feast for the Eyes

Behind the screening hedge, which scratches me,
grasping at itself, an orchard
froths up in white, the umbellifers
have run to seed, they'll harvest
thistle wool here, plucked by the wind,
the heracleums are marauding intruders,
the fruit, considered worthless,
is left to fall, a walker
in wild flight from himself heads
further towards the fermented horizon, just as
another, his senses dulled
under a blanketing haze, sought
the distant land of Elis
and King Augeas of the many herds.

# Taking out the Hives by Knut Ødegaard

introduced and translated by Kenneth Steven

**Knut Ødegaard** was born in the year the Second World War ended. He hails from the west coast of Norway, from a region renowned for its fjord and mountain country.

His first collection of poetry – *Dreamer, Wanderer and Source* – was published when he was just 22 years of age. Since that time he has produced a steady stream of collections and won recognition as one of Norway's foremost poets. His work has been translated into over a dozen tongues. In the course of those long years of writing, his verse has undergone mighty sea changes; the early work is conservative and its tone high, that of his two most recent volumes harsh and exposed to touch the rawness and pain of human suffering.

Ødegaard has been a restless traveller. Iceland in particular has been a home to him, and he has translated the work of a whole series of classical and contemporary Icelandic poets. Nor has he limited himself to the genre of poetry – there have been plays, picture books and novels for teenagers too.

When one meets Knut Ødegaard one is immediately aware of a man interested in every atom of delight existence can furnish him with. He will leap effortlessly from one subject to another with all the efficiency of a Lofoten mountain goat, and his eyes flash as he embarks on a new tack, discusses a new venture, spies a new corner of an old thought. Norwegian artists of all types have a tendency to hide behind their creativity, shrinking away from any possible limelight and seeking always to fit in with the flock. This is particularly true in the strictly Lutheran valleys of the west coast. Knut Ødegaard, with his gaudy neckerchiefs and brimmed hats, breaks all the rules and cocks a snook at the conformists as he does so. He has the genes of Knut Hamsun.

Ødegaard is intensely aware of the sacred, yet he visits the darkest and often the most shocking corners in his determination to sanctify those places. He gets to the quintessential core of the Christian creed to fulfil that mission, celebrating the Christ who came to seek out the lost, the broken and the abandoned.

Knut Ødegaard was instrumental in establishing one of Norway's most important literary events, the Bjørnson Festival. This takes place each summer in his home town of Molde, and is host to many writers both from Scandinavia and far beyond. Alongside readings and performances are hammer-and-tongs debates on the function and future of literature. Knut is almost invariably to be found there himself – if not reading then certainly debating, moving from the sublime to the skittish with a flick of his cigarette.

## We Took the Hives Out There

The heather bloomed best out by the blowy beaches to the west.
We took the hives out there to the sea when the russet clover
was fading inland by the fjord, came with the red-lacquered Ford
that had room for six hives in the boot.
It was all about finding sanctuary from a wind
that's never still here.

When I was a child with dad in the eight-cylinder Ford
  I thought in my child-like way that, as in the song, there lay foxes under
                              the roots of the birches,
as we slowly drove by the dirt tracks west in the evenings
after the worker bees had come into their hives again
their back feet laden with nectar and pollen.

On rainy days we started out sooner, for then the bees
crept about inside with their glistening wings and worked at feeding
                              their larvae
and transforming nectar into honey in cells of wax. Thousands, yes,
perhaps fifty thousand on the move in each of their hives
in the back of the car that dad and I drove out in.

I thought as the car curled softly round the rain-grey fjord
that it must have been great to know Bjørnstjerne Bjørnson. Dad
agreed he must have been
a fine fellow, but that he was dead now. I looked for foxes
but the roots were difficult to see now beneath the birches
from the car windows – they flickered by, and after we'd come further
                              out towards the sea
their trunks were thinner and wild chervil grew in the ditches
and feet-high foxgloves with ringed bells of purple
before we came out to the fields of heather.

It was in one of the thunder summers I thought such thoughts in the
                                        Ford. Lightning
flickered across the sky, but we murmured in the downpour afterwards,
                            mostly about Bjørnson. Dad steered
and I sat and pumped small clouds of smoke into the back of the car
towards bees that crept from impossible cracks.

When we stopped by some rocks in the heather it was a case of not
                                                slipping
among the roots and mud and wet stones as we bore out hives
                                                humming
from the boot of the Ford and up the path to where they could stand
                                        sheltered from the wind
from the sea. I got the wild scent of wax and honey in my nostrils
as I bore the hive close to my child's chest and neck; I sensed
the bees boiling on the inner wall of the hive. The song about the fox
                                        under the birch roots
was swelling within me in the cloudburst that followed the lightning
that split the Atlantic in two, as in the Bible, and a bull-like rumbling
                                                        arose
from the ocean depths, and spread over the coast where dad and I
                                        stood furthest out,
a beehive between us.

Thus: dad and I, yoked together, with fifty thousand bees crawling
                                        about in the hive
we held, while heaven and earth were ripped to shreds about us. As we
                                        stood there
in our boots, and the storm drove in over the land towards
                                        Trollheimen,
Hallingskarvet and Sweden, we set the hives in the heather,
went down to the car and fetched the others.
Our feet had found a fine rhythm now, and I considered that
                            Bjørnstjerne Bjørnson too
had been a boy here, and had thought about foxes under the birch
                                                roots
further in by the fjord.

We put on our protective headgear with veils that fell down
over our shoulders, and secured all the zips in the trousers
and jackets of those white protective suits,
until we might have been from some American film about creatures
                                                    from outer space
who land on earth – one large and one little creature. I had the task
of pumping the smoke; I broke off small pieces of charcoal which I
                                                dropped into the smoker
and lit with a match. The smoke billowed till dad removed the boards
that covered the mouths of the hives, and the bees streamed out –
at first they kept in clouds in the air above the hives

then all at once one group veered off, out over the heather
while the others descended to the hives
or crawled about on our protective suits. We stood utterly still, dad
and myself, out there by the shore against the ocean that August night,
                                                        seeing the bees
coming back like bright pillars beneath the rainbow spanned out huge
                                                            above us.

We saw them drift down to their respective hives and hover, their
                                        wings like wheels in the air –
just inches over the roofs of the hives – hover a few seconds
before rising in great rings over the hives
and moving slowly in the same great dance out towards the honey-wet
                                                            heather,
swarm after swarm following, a hum over the whole of the heavens.

# Three Uncollected Poems by Eugenio Montale
introduced and translated by Simon Carnell and Erica Segre

**Montale** once described the writing of his poems as a 'waiting on the miracle'. The manuscripts of some of his most celebrated work reveal few marks of revision, and his first three books were composed with scant residue of excluded work: published but 'uncollected' poems; unfinished fragments; miracles that didn't quite happen. The poems which we have translated here are among early exceptions, and as such provide a rare view of near-misses in the development of his first mature style. 'Letter from Levante' (1923) and 'In The Void' (1924) might have been included in the first edition of *Ossi di sepia* (1925), whereas 'The sweet years…' (1926) would have been in contention for its second edition in 1927.

The earliest poem in *Ossi di sepia* was composed, according to its author, 'completely entire, with its prey attached'. That 'prey', as he went on to explain, 'was, quite obviously, my personal landscape'. This personal landscape consists partly of Eastern Liguria and the Cinque Terre, with its 'barren, rough, hallucinatory beauty' (not 'the coast of Tuscany', as a recent translation of his work has it) and partly of a landscape which is altogether more slanted, interiorised and peculiar. Though hardly a regional writer in any narrow sense of the term, Montale wrote of the Ligurian setting of *Ossi* that he was 'trying to write a line that would adhere to every fibre of that soil'. This faithfulness with regard to an actual, given ground was bound up with an urgency towards linguistic modernism: to 'wring the neck of the eloquence of our old aulic language' , and it's a critical commonplace that the principal 'neck' in question was that of D'Annunzio – perhaps in particular the D'Annunzio of *Alcyone*, a widely read sequence chronicling a summer spent on the Tuscan coast. Where D'Annunzio had been classicising and altitudinous, Montale would take the language down off its stilts, roughen its music, and clear too obviously received literary props and properties from view. And where he had been awash with declared emotion and panegyric, Montale would treat the poem as an object which should emit emotion rather than explicitly declare or comment upon it.

'Letter from Levante' is Montale's single longest attempt to 'adhere to the soil' of Liguria in the light of this project. Stylistically it is located in a borderland between the reticence and compression of his so-called 'poetry of the object', and some of the relatively spacious poems of *Ossi*. Even compared to the latter it contains more connective tissue, direct statement and epistolary latitude – and contrasts with those poems in the first volume which have already begun to function by eliminating links in a chain of intricately and rapidly associated parts, and to suppress the occasion of the poem whilst plunging the reader *in medias res*. It also intrigues as an early, extended example of the poem levelled at an unnamed female addressee - a 'genre' which would prove crucial to its author's work. Though it's easy see how it did not otherwise conform to the direction in which Montale's work was moving, it has intrinsic value as a revealing and moving love poem. With its combination of clear-cut images, abrupt movement and obscure sense of unease and stasis; with its finding in a faithfulness to appearances a sudden drop behind or beyond the visible, 'In the Void' will probably strike anyone familiar with Montale as more characteristically successful. The single, tightly wound and involved sentence which comprises 'The sweet years...' and contains one of those strangely memorable Montalean 'signs' drawn from the natural world ('the liquid darting of a tarantula/on a flaking wall') was eventually preserved by its author, along with the 'Letter' and 'In the Void', in a late volume which appeared as a series of appendices in the definitive, posthumous *Tutte le poesie*.

## Letter from Levante

I'd like these syllables,
that with a hesitant schoolboy hand
I trace with difficulty,
to reach you on a dark day
of  boredom – when noon
yields no other sound
than that of a melting eave,
and not a single conviction
survives the corrosive moment,
and the spotless white walls face us,
the horror of living rising in the throat.

Then you're sure to remember
the companion of many hours spent
on brick-paved walkways
that cut, closely hugging the dips and inclines,
our dwarfish hills dressed
in the ragged lace of bare branches.
It will seem as if you're no longer running
alone beneath the ruffled canopies
of olives, with abrupt stops and starts,
shrunk in an eye-blink to child-size.
Your memory will fill
with the trees we knew:
bearded palms and leafy cedars.
And your beloved medlars.

This is the memory I'd like to leave
in your life:
to be the loyal shadow that accompanies,
asking nothing for itself;
the image that emerges from the foxed print
of childhood recall, and creates a still moment
in the day's turbulence.
And if at times an invisible power
has you in a web
of burning hours,
Oh briefly imagine
that you're secretly taken by the hand.
Not by some angel of edifying lore,
but by your unobtrusive friend.

Keep listening. I want to reveal
the thread that joins our separate lives,
how even if you're silent I can hear, almost,
the shadows and transparencies of your voice.
One day you told me of a childhood spent
amongst your hunting father's
owls and dogs – and from then on I thought
you were in touch with the essence
of things, the root system
of life's frondiferous plants.
So while your contemporaries
spent their days blithely
at play, or amongst the hour's
anxieties, indolently,
with your few although unblemished
autumns, friend, you'd already
glimpsed the key
to the mystery which weaves us.

I, too, often in my rustic
Levantine adolescence
would climb quickly before dawn
to the rocky summit to see the first sun,
companions by my side
with sunburnt faces.
Silently balancing in our hands
ancient arquebuses,
we advanced in the darkness,
occasionally stopping
to measure with our fingers
the black gunpowder and the vetch
trampled at the base of canes.
I waited sunk in a bush
for the long ring
of wild doves
to rise from the smoking vales
of olive groves
and turn towards the summit
of the mountain –
now in shadow, now lit.
Slowly I aimed at the stranded grey
leader of the line, pulled the trigger;
in the blue the sharp report
was like breaking glass.

The struck bird veered, gave to the air
a few tufts of feathers, and came down
like a wind-blown piece of paper.
All around a mad beating of wings.
Then sudden silence.

And I discovered further in my early
days, observing
the hare killed in the low vines
or the rust-coloured squirrel that carries
its tail like a red torch
from pine to pine,
that those small scrubland creatures
sometimes carry for months
the minute lead shot
in healed wounds in their sides,
until a weightier bullet
brings them to earth for good.

Perhaps I digress; but only because
thoughts of myself and memories of you
trigger scenes of wounded animals;
because I cannot think
of our disparate lives
without visceral recall
of sensations that are primal
and of images that stand
before the difficulty
of living that's now our lot.
Oh I understand and you sense it
too; more than the fancy
that kins us with wind and trees,
more than nostalgia for an azure sky
imprinted on our gaze;
what unites us is our old
shared presentiment:
of being wounded by a world
that's obscurely maleficent.

We met as if coming together again
after long years of wandering,
the spool of time unwinding
for us an endless thread.
Side by side we walked without surprise,
without masks, with plain words.
I think of certain past times
when the return of light or end of day
so tormented me
I didn't know with whom I'd ever share
my rich heaviness – yet all around
sensed the flowing of a benevolent power,
a bond of friendship unexpectedly emerge,
between myself and another.

I sense that in those moments
you were already by my side, are there still
though far away, in this guttering day
ending without apotheosis.
And that together we watch fade,
among the breakers and the dense mists,
the cliffs of the Cinque Terre
whipped by foaming wave-crests.


### In the Void

The sun's mane caught
in the cane stakes of the vegetable plots –
on the shore, seeming to doze, the odd lifeboat.

The day yielded no sound
beneath the polished arch,
not even a pine cone's thud
or bud's detonation,
on the other side of the walls.

Silence swallowed everything.
Our boat hadn't stopped,
cut the sand like razor wire; a sign long hovering in air
plummeted.

Now the earth was an overflowing rim,
weight melted in the glare,
the blaze that was the dark's foam,
the pit widening, too deep
for us and for anchors.
                              Until suddenly
something happened, the trench sealed
shut, everything and nothing was lost.
And I was awake to the sound
of your rediscovered lips –
the vein imprisoned
in crystal
which waits to be released.


## 'The sweet years that with long refractions...'

The sweet years that with long refractions
illuminate our latest,
submerged in an overflowing stream;
lost years when adventure
was brushwood crowned
by whirling flights around a field,
or the liquid darting of a tarantula
on a flaking wall;
sweet years that I make out like a faint light
through fog – now that they burn around me
without flame, unceasing
anguish that more and more a north wind re-kindles
thoughts and faces I no longer know,
and meet bewildered;
years which she who sees but doesn't understand
will follow in the nearing coffin
drawn by the vortex that swirls lives
and drags them down
into darkness.

# Reviews

## The Night of Akhenaton
### selected poems of Ágnes Nemes Nagy

translated by George Szirtes with his introduction and an essay by the author, Bloodaxe Books, 2004, ISBN 1 85224 641 3. £8.95

Ágnes Nemes Nagy (1922-1991) is considered in Hungary to be among the nation's most distinguished poets of the post-war years. Born in Budapest, she studied at the Péter Pázmány University, where she first began writing poetry. In the 1970s and 1980s she was a leading figure in the world of Hungarian letters, as well as being awarded several international literary prizes.

The present volume is the third collection of English translations of her work – the previous two by Bruce Berlind (1980) and Hugh Maxton (1988) – and all but a very few of the poems selected by Szirtes are contained in one or both of the others. The lack of new material is regrettable but gives the opportunity of comparing Szirtes's versions with his precursors', while the inclusion of the same poems – and Nemes Nagy's collaboration in all three volumes - indicates that they represent the central core of her work. As a Hungarian who has lived most of his life in England, Szirtes has a foot in both linguistic camps, and as an accredited poet in English he is able to produce versions of higher poetic quality than his predecessors, who knew little or no Hungarian.

In her introductory essay to Berlind's book (here printed as an appendix), Nemes Nagy expounds her poetic philosophy: delight in being a Hungarian poet, in particular the linguistic advantage and social status this confers and belief that the poet is 'a specialist in the emotions', with poetry 'one of the great roads to human cognition'. She is in many respects, a poet's poet; her nature imagery is of the finest:

> The trees, and then the stream behind,
> the wild duck's silent sway of wing,
> the deep blue night, white and blind,
> where stand the hooded tribe of things,
> here one must learn the unsung deeds
> of heroism of the trees.

('Trees')

The tree is a complex symbol in her work; reaching from Earth toward Heaven, it stands for steadfastness and survival against the disappointments in her life, as well as having religious significance as the

Tree on which Christ died. In 'Night Oak', the eponymous tree follows a walker

> up the street at night, who
> stopped and waited for it. The oak
> proceeded dragging on raw roots
> still shedding earth, wriggling long serpentine limbs
> down the metalled road...

The oak, described as 'an awkward mermaid', is evidently female. It has birds' nests in its hair, their sleeping birds 'unaware, unremembered'. After a wordless yet urgent confrontation with the walker it

> Turned round. Set off. Strange-footed.
> It took its nests and birds
> and before the solidifying eyes
> of the night walker
> neon signs sprinkled light on it,
> and melted back into the hole in the ground
> which was ready to receive it.

I am indebted to Judy Kendall for the suggestion that, unlike the oak in Miklós Radnóti's 'First Eclogue', which represents the poet himself, the tree here represents Nagy's work – in which case the night walker must be herself.

Similarly, the title poem recalls the confusion of the bloody events of October/November 1956:

> He leapt across some rails along
> with all the others,
> together they rolled down an embankment,
> piecemeal, jerkily, tumbled
> under continuous gunfire, over each other
> like an avalanche.
>
> ('The Night of Akhenaton')

Again, one wonders whether the third person pronoun in this poem should be feminine (Hungarian does not mark gender), making the poem truly personal. One must find fault, too, with Szirtes's translation of *fent sorozatok még* ( 'up above, automatic-bursts still') as 'under continuous gunfire', a rather different impression.

Criticism can also be levelled at the translation of the poem 'When', in which much of Szirtes's English is not to be found in the taut original. In translating verse there is always the temptation – even the need – to 'pad' for the sake of keeping the original rhyme-scheme or metre, and there is no simple answer to the question of how closely one should follow form, although certainly not to the point of distorting the sense, however pleasing to the ear the result may seem. The translator should also avoid inappropriate dialectal words ('. . . rotting rags and *clout*') or archaisms ('. . . when Thespis *prinks*') which appear now and then in Szirtes' versions. It is easy to criticise minutiae, but when so much of the translation is so good such things are conspicuous.

Nemes Nagy's work is profound - readers must not expect 'an easy read' - although they will see its subtlety for themselves. In the forefront of Hungarian letters from 1957 onwards, her output was relatively small. Though she may have been 'too distant, too unbending, too disdainful of popularity' to be a popular writer, her influence on her successors has been considerable. Her originality and poetic power have made her a symbol of her generation, and whatever may be lost in translation her appearance in this slim volume is to be welcomed.

**Bernard Adams**

*Absurd Athlete* by **Yannis Kondos**
translated by David Connolly and introduced by David Constantine
(Arc Publications: Visible Poets no. 11, 2003, 110pp., £8.95) ISBN 1
900072 76 9

Yannis Kondos's work grows out of thematic and stylistic shifts initiated by the so-called 'generation of the 70s' that saw Greek poets moving towards more metaphysical, personal spheres from where rapid social changes are often observed.

Translated by David Connolly, *Absurd Athlete*, his tenth collection and recipient of the 1997 State Prize for Poetry, appears in Arc's *Visible Poets* series, perhaps one of the healthiest platforms for a European poet to be eased towards English readership; extended translator's prefaces help to recognize the critical and creative roles of mediating subjectivity, while introductions by some of our most prominent literary figures celebrate the otherness of foreign literature for the precious lifeblood it always has been. It all points to a shift in publishing mores for translated poetry, and, as such, one hopes it will find many imitators.

Kondos's poetry trails the diaspora of experience in hectic city routines, lingering on commonplaces, going for the openings when life coincides with its reflection. His work is distinctly synaesthetic ('I unfold

my patience. / It's woollen and brownish / Time is striped.') and the
surreal quickenings he injects to his warm, colloquial language help to
arrest the reality behind life's absurdities, arriving time and again at the
everyday recognitions that already are the stuff of poetry. It gives these
poems an organic, decided feel as they leap, effortlessly almost, from the
humdrum to the sublime:

> The sun pierces the cupboards and chests
> and the moth slips in. It makes furrows
> in the mind, in the blankets that cover you
> in winter. Winter's in the storeroom
> waiting. Everything's waiting for
> the earth to suck the trees' saps,
> for the trees to sleep,
> for us to wake.
> For the moment, we're hunting bugs and ideas.
> We don't hunt our shadow,
> because it's become a crowd watching us.
>
> 'Summertime'

He is also not averse to fashioning narratives out of our little dramas,
often embedding contemporary theatre and film ('he never imagined he'd
become / a character out of Samuel Beckett.'; 'Summer, like in a play /
by Tennessee Williams.'; 'It could be a Bergman film') into his stagings of
modern alienation. The approach is strongly visual (indeed 'film shorts'
could be a two-word review of this book) in making us *see*, yet the inner
space witnessed relies on poetic insight: 'It's raining again and you kiss me
indifferently / gazing over my shoulder / at the next days jostling / in the
doorway'. Given the subject matter (*tempus fugit*, death is omnipresent, a
sense of not being at one with oneself), Kondos's penchant for irony
both intensifies the effect of his often dark verse, yet at the same time
lends it a nod of assent in the face of everyday anxieties. Along with his
knack for telling a story, it also adds much to the enjoyment of this
poetry.

As for the translation, it is a beautiful match between the *Visible Poets*
setting and Connolly's own meticulous approach; his inventive and
intelligent renderings bear out his reputation as one of the most
dependable translators a Greek writer could wish for and afford this
series one of its most rewarding volumes so far. And although publishing realities and our own need to catch up might more often necessitate
the jet-lag of a volume of selected or collected poems of translated literature, it is refreshing, if not downright vital, to be confronted with
translations of recent single collections that make it possible to follow
modern world poetry closer to real time. In acquainting us with Greek

poetry as it is happening now, books like *Absurd Athlete* can only be welcomed as steps in the right direction.

**Paschalis Nikolaou**

## Georg Heym *Poems*
translated, with an introduction and notes by Antony Hasler
216pp. Libris. £30 (pb £14.95) 1 870352874

It was once memorably stated of Chopin's late 'Polonaises' that they were like the confessions of a man with his throat cut. One might say the same of the poetry of Georg Heym, which, following decades of woeful neglect, is at last made available to us in exemplary translations by Antony Hasler. Heym who died in 1912 in the most dreadful circumstances, aged only twenty four, was an unswerving romantic, an intensely subjective poet who though presenting a rowdy and devil-may-care image on the outside was internally blessed with acute sensibilities and a prolific lyricism. This lyrical greatness became even more significant in his later work, in poems which, profoundly influenced by Hölderlin, have secured Heym a permanent place in the front row of German language poets. Though Heym is often dubbed an 'Expressionist' poet, as with his better known contemporary Trakl, this labels proves far too simplistic.

Georg Heym was born in 1887, the son of a Prussian military officer. His relationship with his father was unfulfilling and remained unresolved until his death, and his mother failed to understand her son's burgeoning vocation. Like the Austrian painter Egon Schiele, Heym had little time for his teachers and academia, and was scathing in his contempt for the establishment in general. Highly volatile and with a surplus of rude vitality, the young Heym led a restless bohemian existence in Berlin, chasing an endless stream of girls with disturbing excesses of passion. He suffered chronic mood swings, and, craving decisive change, entertained notions of escaping to far-flung lands or indulged in suicidal fantasies. His thoughts were inscribed in a remarkable diary, sadly not yet translated into English. Antony Hasler summarises thus: 'His diaries show continuing melancholy and turbulence, and a highly fertile dream life which he records with merciless detachment.'

To begin with, Heym tried his hand at drama but his efforts were snubbed by publishers. However, after getting a chance to read his work at the fashionable *Neuer Club* in Berlin, presided over by Jacob Von Hoddis and a regular haunt for the likes of Karl Kraus, Else Lasker-

Schüler and Gottfried Benn, his incendiary poems soon began to appear in journals and a first collection *Der Ewige Tag* was published in 1911. As Patrick Bridgwater affirms in his valuable biography, every single one of Heym's many heroes was a thorough romantic and/or revolutionary. As early as 1905 Heym declares a deep fraternal bond with Hölderlin, this is extended in 1908-9 to Kleist and Büchner, uncompromising romantic spirits who died young. In this respect, Shelley and Keats were also to draw the young Heym's gaze. Baudelaire, Rimbaud and Verlaine all followed. Büchner's drama *Dantons Tod* aroused Heym's fascination for the French Revolution. In the poem 'Robespierre', one of a series on this theme, Hasler manages to retain the original rhyme scheme and produce something which reads convincingly in English without resorting to jarring embellishments. Although assonance has had to be drafted in, it sits comfortably alongside the full rhymes.

### Robespierre

He bleats, but in his throat. The bland eyes stare
into the tumbril's straw. Sucking, he draws
the white phlegm through his teeth from chewing jaws.
Between two wooden struts a foot hangs bare.

At every jolt the wagon flings him up.
The fetters on his arms rattle like bells.
Mothers hoist their children up, and yells
of cheerful laughter cross the rabble's top.

Someone tickles his leg. He does not see.
The wagon stops. He looks up. At the end
of the street he sees the last black penalty.

Upon the ash-grey brow the cold sweat stands.
And in the face the mouth twists fearfully.
They wait for screams. But no one hears a sound.

This shocking poem exhibits details of the real visually enhanced by the imagination, and it is this revelatory synthesis which is surely crucial to Heym's vision. We are there with Robespierre (and Heym?) in the tumbril and feel acutely the supreme terror of his fate. Thus details like the 'tickling of a leg' or the 'cheerful laughter' drifting over the rabble hold the most mordant significance.

Like Baudelaire who seems to be eerily present in the above poem, Heym farms a no-man's land between the disquieting image based on truth and subjective lyrical impulse. Following Kirchner, perhaps his painterly brother, Heym sought the concealed truths of the metropolis in ferment, the sprawling moloch of Berlin. Poems like 'The Fever Hospital', 'The Morgue' and 'The Slums' are relentless in their morbid delirium. Heym seeks to distil the mayhem, pretension, emptiness and diabolism of the modern city. His most famous poems such as 'The Demons of the City' and 'War' are vessels for metaphorical abandon , crammed with apocalyptic images, and reminiscent of the scenes of skeleton-supervised human carnage in Brueghel's famous painting 'The Triumph of Death'. It is not surprising to learn that Heym, essentially a visual poet, revered Van Gogh, Munch, Kubin and Rops, poet-painters who shadow each other in their visionary excesses.

Hasler understands that Heym's power is forged through the combination of haunting image and the melody scored by his remorseless iambic pentameters. Once a translator has placed his wheel in the tramline so to speak and adopted a formal rhyme scheme, it proves impossible to deviate and he/she must continue until the end. For many translators a spectacular crash is inevitable. In these translations one senses genuine poetic sensitivity at work, not just the tricks of a canny craftsman. And as has been demonstrated, where he does not manage to rhyme convincingly he compensates with a seemingly inexhaustible reserve of intuitive assonance. In all respects Hasler's patient labour serves as an invaluable lesson to any prospective translator of poetry.

Heym's language is breathless and forever in a frenzy of motion. Forests 'rise and climb', dusk 'rushes upwards', the sea 'gulps'. Heym takes the moon as a symbol again and again. In one poem alone he comes up with eight different metaphors for the moon. In another the moon 'lifts up its swinging lamp', or 'monstrous moons heave themselves stiff-legged over the rooftops', 'before his eyes a green half moon leads dances…' Behind the frantic symbolism, Heym's single unifying theme is death, and, like Trakl, he is overwhelmingly impelled towards morbid imagery. Trakl's mournful cry that 'All roads lead to blackest carrion' also resonates in the poetry of Heym. Michael Hofmann has referred to this ghoulish preoccupation as a 'typically Germanic mixture of bleakness and luridness, a frail, self-imperilled, insatiable nature; and a poetry dwelling obsessively on death and decay, narrowly and culpably pathognomic'.

But Heym, again like Trakl, can also surprise with a wave of serene beauty or tenderness. This is most evident in a remarkable short prose piece 'The Autopsy' included in the wonderful collection of short stories also published by Libris. Although a man's corpse is seized on by doctors and systematically violated by chisels, scalpels and hammers, the flame of love still burns somewhere deep within, and the corpse recalls tender moments with his beloved amidst the gruesome hacking and sawing. The result is a minor masterpiece. Such deliberate incongruity also pays off in the poem 'The Dead Girl in the Water', in which the corpse of a girl floats out on the tide from the city. The imagery created here by Heym is both sumptuous and harrowing. Here are three consecutive stanzas.

The body wallows up, inflates the dress
as if it were a white ship in the wind.
The lifeless eyes stare up, enormous, blind,
into a sky of cloud-pink rosiness.

The lilac water gently rocks and swells,
the wake stirred by the water-rats, who man
the white ship. Now it drifts serenely on,
writhing with grey snouts and with dusky pelts.

In bliss the dead girl rides the outward draw
of wind and tide, her swollen belly heaving,
big, hollowed out, all that the rats are leaving.
It murmurs like a grotto as they gnaw.

and the German of the first of those stanzas:

Die Leiche wälzt sich ganz heraus. Es bläht
Das Kleid sich wie ein weisses Schiff im Wind.
Die toten Augen starren gross und blind
Zum Himmel, der voll rosa Wolken steht.

A return to Hölderlin in 1912 and an upsurge of controlled lyrical power delivered new shorter-line poems of greater range and emotional reach. Works like 'Autumn Tetralogy' and 'Umbra Vitae' are considered perhaps the pinnacle of Heym's achievement, whilst 'Your Eyelashes, Long' is a love poem of considerable depth and emotive power. But soon after this, tragedy struck and Heym was gone. In 1910 he had noted in eerie detail a dream he had of his death by drowning. On a winter's day in 1912 this dream was to become a ghastly reality, when on a skating expedition on the Havel with his friend Ernst Balcke, the two fell through the ice and were drowned.

**Will Stone**

# Further Books Received

*Basho's Haiku: Selected Poems of Matsuo Basho,* translated with an introduction by David Landis Barnhill, State University of New York Press, $23.95, pp331, ISBN: 0 7914 6166 1

Jean Boase-Beier, Alexandra Büchler & Fiona Sampson (eds), *A Fine Line: New Poetry from Central & Eastern Europe,* Arc, £11.95, pp 268, ISBN: 1 90007 297 1

Gabriel Ferrater, *Women and Days,* translated by Arthur Terry, introduced by Seamus Heaney, Arc Visible Poets, £8.95, pp96, ISBN: 1 9000072 90 4

Celia de Fréine, *Fiacha Fola,* Cló Iar-Chonnachta, €10, pp88, ISBN: 1 902420 88 8

Mila Haugová, *Scent of the Unseen,* translated by James & Viera Sutherland-Smith, introduction by Fiona Sampson, Arc Visible Poets, £8.95, pp136, ISBN 1 900072 39 4

Peter Huchel, *The Garden of Theophrastus,* translated by Michael Hamburger, Anvil, £10.95, pp207, ISBN: 0 85646 344 2

Diarmuid Johnson, *Súil Saoir,* Cló Iar-Chonnachta, €10, pp117, ISBN: 1 902420 70 5

Jaan Kaplinski, *Evening Brings Everything Back,* translated by Jaan Kaplinski with Fiona Sampson, Bloodaxe Books, £ 8.95, pp95, ISBN: 1 85224 650 2

Bejan Matur, *In the Temple of a Patient God,* translated by Ruth Christie, introduction by Maureen Freely, Arc Visible Poets, £9.95, pp132, ISBN: 1 900072 96 3

Ernst Meister, *Between Nothing and Nothing,* translated by Jean Boase-Beier, introduction by John Hartley Williams, £8.95, pp127, ISBN: 1 900072 38 6

Anzhelina Polonskaya, *A Voice: Selected Poems,* edited and translated by Andrew Wachtel, Northwestern University Press, $14.95, pp67, ISBN: 0 8101 2089 5

Jan Twardowski, *Serious Angel: A Selection of Poems,* translated by Sarah Lawson & Makgorzata Koraszewska, Dedalus, Waxwing Series, £7.95, pp32, ISBN: 1 90455 617 5

Daniel Weissbort, *From Russian with Love: Joseph Brodsky in English,* Anvil, £12.95, pp254, ISBN: 0 85646 342 6

# Notes on Contributors

**Bernard Adams** read Hungarian and Russian at Cambridge, had a career in teaching (mostly at Highgate School), and took early retirement in 1991 to concentrate on Hungarian literary translation. His published work includes Zsigmond Móricz's *Relations,* Tibor Cseres's *Cold Days,* and the autobiographies of Katalin and Miklós Bethlen.

**Paul Batchelor** was born in Northumberland. His poems and reviews have appeared in *Poetry Wales* and *Poetry Review.* Last year he was given an Eric Gregory award. He is currently studying for a PhD on the poetry of Barry MacSweeney at Newcastle University.

**Carmen Bugan** is the author of *Crossing the Carpathians* (OxfordPoets/Carcanet 2004), and an editor of *Oxford Poetry.* Her poems and prose have appeared in *PN Review, The TLS, Magma* and elsewhere. She wrote a doctoral thesis at Oxford University on the poetry of Seamus Heaney.

**Tom Cheesman** is an academic and runs Hafan Books, the publishing arm of Swansea Bay Asylum Seekers Support Group. He translates poetry and fiction from German and French.

**John Goodby** is a poet and academic, author of a collection of poems, *A Birmingham Yank* (Arc, 1998), and *Irish poetry since 1950: from stillness into history* (Manchester University Press, 2000) and the *New Casebook on Dylan Thomas* (2001).

**George Gömöri** is a native of Hungary who has been living in England since 1956. He is a retired lecturer of the University of Cambridge. Apart from nine books of verse in Hungarian, he has published one book of poetry in English: *My Manifold City*,1996, 2nd ed.1998) and several books of translations from the Hungarian with Clive Wilmer, the last of which was Miklós Radnóti's *Forced March* (Enitharmon, 2003).

**Yvonne Green** read law at the L.S.E., practised as a commercial barrister for 20 years, and has now retired to publish the poems she has always written. Poems of hers have appeared in *The Jewish Quarterly*, *Poetry Review*, *The Interpreter's House* and elsewhere.

**David Harsent's** last collection *Marriage* was shortlisted for both the T.S.Eliot and Forward prizes. *Sprinting From the Graveyard* was his English versions of poems written by the Bosnian poet Goran Simic while under siege in Sarajevo. He was co-editor, with Mario Suško, of *Savremena Britanska Poezija*, an anthology of British and Irish poetry commissioned by the Sarajevo Writers' Union. Harsent's new collection, *Legion*, will appear from Faber & Faber next spring. He has collaborated with a number of composers, most notably with Harrison Birtwistle, and is currently at work on a libretto, *Minotaur*, for Birtwistle and the Royal Opera House.

**Olivia McCannon** is a writer and translator, based in Paris. Her poems and short stories have been awarded prizes, broadcast on BBC radio and published in, for example, *Ambit* and the *Oxford Magazine*. Her translation work includes French and Cuban plays for the Royal Court, and a new version of Balzac's *Old Goriot* for Penguin.

**Paschalis Nikolaou** has an Onassis Foundation scholarship at the University of East Anglia where he is completing a doctoral thesis on the interface of literary translation, creativity and autobiography. He is currently working on translations of the poets Richard Burns and Nasos Vayenas.

**Gholamreza Sami Gorgan Roodi** received his Ph.D from the University of Sussex in England where he is currently a researcher. He taught Comparative Literature at various Iranian Universities before coming to England in 1999 and has published many articles on modern Persian and English Literatures in Iranian and British Journals. His current research is on the representation of Persia in English and American literatures.

Erica Segre is a native Italian speaker and fellow in Spanish at Trinity College, Cambridge. Simon Carnell has published poems in the *TLS, LRB, Poetry Review, Harvard Review,* and elsewhere. Their co-translations of poems by Montale, Ungaretti and Quasimodo were included in the recent *Faber Book of 20th-Century Italian Poetry.*

Goran Simic is one of the most prominent writers of the former Yugoslavia. He has published eleven volumes of poetry, drama and short fiction, among them *Sprinting from the Graveyard* (1997), an account of the siege of Sarajevo, and *Immigrant Blues* (2003). He is the recipient of a PEN Freedom to Write Award. In 1996 he and his family settled in Canada.

Kenneth Steven is a poet, translator and children's author from Perthshire in Scotland. He spent two academic years in Norway, one on the west coast and the other north of the Arctic Circle. In 2002 he was commissioned by Arcadia Books to translate the Nordic Prize-winning Norwegian novel *The Half Brother* by Lars Saabye Christensen. This was published in the spring of 2003 and the translation was subsequently short-listed for the Foreign Fiction Prize. Recently it was nominated for the International IMPAC Literary Award.

Will Stone was born in 1966 and lives in Suffolk. His work has appeared in *Agenda, London Magazine, TLS, Poetry Salzburg, The International Review* and other journals. His *Selected Poems of Georg Trakl* will appear from Arc in 2005.

Stefan Tobler was born in Belem, Brazil in 1974. He is a translator from Portuguese and German. His poetry translations have appeared in various UK and US journals and magazines, such as *The Rialto, Poetry Wales* and *Ambit.* He is also a member of the group that translates collaboratively at the Poetry Translation Centre at SOAS.

Stephen Watts is a poet, editor and translator. He co-edited *Voices Of Conscience* (1995), *Mother Tongues* (2001) (an anthology of 'Non English-Language Poetry In England'), and *Music While Drowning* (2003). His selected poems *The Blue Bag* (Aark Arts, Delhi & London) was published in 2004. In addition to contemporary Persian poets, he is co-translating the poetry of A. N Stencl from Yiddish and Meta Kusar from Slovenian. He runs writing workshops in schools & hospitals, and lives in Whitechapel, in East London. His own poetry has been translated into several languages including Ziba Karbassi's translations of his work into

Persian, and he has compiled extensive bibliographies of modern poetry in English translation.

**Clive Wilmer** has published five books of his own poetry, the most recent of which is *The Falls* (Worple, 2000). He has translated many poems from the Hungarian in collaboration with George Gomori; their most recent book is the revised and enlarged edition of Miklös Radnöti's **Forced March** (Enitharmon, 2003).

**Elzbieta Wójcik-Leese** co-edited the bilingual anthology *Carnivorous Boy and Carnivorous Bird: Poetry from Poland* (Zephyr Press, 2004). Her translations of contemporary Polish poets have appeared in Britain, America and Nepal (*Selected Poets of Modern Europe, 2004*). Her English versions of Kielar's poems are forthcoming from Zephyr Press in 2006.

**MODERN POETRY IN TRANSLATION. Series 3 Number 1**

*INTRODUCTIONS*

**Edited by David and Helen Constantine**

Cover by Chris Hyde

**Contents**

Editorial     David and Helen Constantine

# THE TRANSLATORS ASSOCIATION

The Translators Association (TA) was formed in 1958 to provide support to translators of published works, and to promote the highest standards of literary translation. It is a subsidiary group of the Society of Authors, a trade union for professional writers with over 7,000 members. To qualify for membership of the TA a translator must have had one full-length work, or its equivalent, published or accepted for publication. Each application is considered on its own merits.

Benefits of membership include:

- **Contract Vetting**
  On receipt of your first year's membership subscription our expert staff will give confidential, clause by clause advice on the terms of your contract, before you return it to your publisher.
- **Advice on Copyright**
  The TA will advise on copyright, accountancy, tax and libel matters.
- **Support with problems and disputes**
  The TA will take up complaints for members and, in certain circumstances, may undertake legal proceedings.
- *In Other Words* and *The Author*
  These journals are sent free to all members of the TA. They provide invaluable sources of information on all aspects of the business of writing and translating, including surveys on publishers and features on issues currently of concern to the profession.
- **Opportunities to meet other translators and to attend practical workshops**
- **Links with international organisations**
- **Automatic membership of the ALCS**
  You will receive fees from photocopying and other uses of copyright material, handled collectively by the Authors' Licensing and Collecting Society (ALCS).

The annual subscription of the Society is £80 and also covers membership of the TA. The TA has its own Executive Committee which plans meetings and works to increase the status of the profession.

The Society has published a series of Quick Guides and papers, available free to members, including Publishing Contracts, Electronic Publishing Contracts, Copyright and Moral Rights, and Literary Translation, and the TA has produced its own Model Translator/Publisher Agreement.

For further details please contact *Dorothy Sym*, Secretary, Translators Association, The Society of Authors, 84 Drayton Gardens, London SW10 9SB. Tel 020 7373 6642, email info@societyofauthors.org